The Many Faces of
JESSE JAMES

Also by Phillip W. Steele

The Last Cherokee Warriors, 1974

Ozark Tales and Superstitions, 1983

Jesse and Frank James:
The Family History, 1987

Starr Tracks: Belle and Pearl Starr, 1989

Outlaws and Gunfighters of the Old West, 1991

Civil War in the Ozarks, 1993
(coauthored with Steve Cottrell)

The Many Faces of

JESSE JAMES

Phillip W. Steele with George Warfel

PELICAN PUBLISHING COMPANY

Gretna 1995

The word "Pelican" and the depiction of a pelican are trademarks
of Pelican Publishing Company, Inc.,
and are registered in the U.S. Patent and Trademark Office.

Library of Congress Cataloging-in-Publication Data

Steele, Phillip W.
    The many faces of Jesse James / Phillip W. Steele, with George
Warfel.
        p.   cm.
    Includes bibliographical references (p.   ) and index.
    ISBN 1-56554-097-2
    1. James, Jesse, 1847-1882. 2. James, Jesse, 1847-1882—Pictorial
works. 3. Outlaws—West (U.S.)—Biography. I. Warfel, George,
1918- . II. Title.
F594.J27S74 1995
364.1'552'092—dc20
    [B]
                                                                94-45397
                                                                CIP

Manufactured in the United States of America
Published by Pelican Publishing Company, Inc.
1101 Monroe Street, Gretna, Louisiana 70053

Dedicated to the memory
of
James historians
Milton F. Perry
August 14, 1926–August 20, 1991
and
William A. Settle, Jr.
August 20, 1915–March 1, 1988

The Man of Many Faces

Icy pale blue eyes had he,
This man they called Jesse,
With granite jaw and mouth set grim,
No mirth appeared to be within.

Impassive as the Sphinx seems he
In the photos that we see
Printed in our Western books.
How deceiving someone often looks.

But both friend and foe agree,
He was jolly as could be,
Laughed and joked without a care,
Kind, friendly, and debonair.

As faceted as a fly's eye,
He would laugh and then would cry.
Could go to church with brother Frank,
The next day rob a savings bank.

He would aid someone in need,
Thus performing one kind deed.
Then when holding up a train,
Send a bullet through a brain.

These many faces came about,
When as a farm boy he found out
Just how cruel that man can be,
When he assumes authority.

As a lad, yanked from a plough,
Flogged because he wouldn't bow
To Yankee tyrants on a spree
Who hanged his father from a tree.

He went to war—fought for a cause,
Then accused of breaking laws,
Became an outlaw, fierce and bold,
Yet with a heart, so we've been told.

A brother murdered, mother maimed,
Lawmen later to be blamed
For the bomb they tossed inside
Their home in which poor Archie died.

Yes, many faces wore Jesse.
To wear them kept him safe and free
'Til lawmen hired two men with tack
To shoot poor Jesse in the back.

Two-faced killers hired by the law
Behind his back had nerve to draw
On the man with many faces
Whose deck of life ran out of aces.

Many faces we may wear
If faced with danger and despair.
So mock not lions whose pretense
As kittens serve in their defense.

GEORGE LESTER WARFEL
March 10, 1994

Contents

Preface

Those who share your authors' sincere interest in exploring the true story of Jesse James will hopefully find this text helpful in separating the facts of his life from the volumes of fiction created about him by early newspaper and dime novel writers. The real and only Jesse Woodson James, robber of banks, trains, and stagecoaches without ever being arrested, died more than 112 years ago, yet his story remains fresh and new to millions around the world. One might assume that after all of this time and his story having been told in thousands of articles and books, little else is left to write about. Yet, new facts, photographs, and details about the life and times of Jesse James are still emerging and will most likely continue to do so.

The simple fact that the name Jesse James is perhaps the most recognized of any individual in American history is in itself phenomenal. Numerous reasons for his popularity as an American folk hero exist, but the main reason seems to be that he stood for a cause and resisted the tyranny and injustices that were brought to bear against those who had supported the South during the Civil War. Not only had their life-style and homes been destroyed, those who had ridden with the Quantrill guerilla forces during the war were stripped of all their rights as American citizens. No longer could such men ever vote in elections, borrow money from banking institutions, hold public office, or even serve in leadership positions within their churches. A victim of the social environment in which he lived, Jesse James fought back and, in doing so, became a national celebrity. Had Jesse James never existed, Americans would have created him out of a desperate need for a rebellious hero, a champion who would resist the injustices of a corrupt government. It is a tendency for most people to support the innocent underdog when they regard him as a victim of tyranny. Medieval society demanded a Robin Hood, and at that point in our nation's history, we required a Jesse James.

Certainly his name is a romantic one. Certainly a nation's folk hero would have been created had Jesse James not lived. But one wonders if so much literature would have been inspired and new works such as this would continue to be published had his name been Bob Jones or Bill Smith. James R. Ross, Superior Court Judge of Orange County, California, and the great-grandson of Jesse James, once commented, "Considering the destruction of a way of life the Civil War caused the James family and the flagrant discrimination federal authority placed on ex-guerilla members, I might have been the same as Jesse."

Furthermore, it seems that those personalities most often written about in western literature are those who were shot in the back. America despises a coward. The fact Jesse James was shot in the back of the head for a meager $10,000 reward by a "friend" who was afraid to face him further created international sentiment for Jesse James. Belle Starr, John Wesley Hardin, Wild Bill Hickock, Billy the Kid, and other noted personalities have enjoyed literary appeal as a result of their being shot from behind. Jesse James by far excels all others in American history in popularity. We are, therefore, hereby presenting still another volume dealing with this man.

As a result of the international popularity enjoyed by Jesse James, thousands of family researchers continue to go to great lengths to prove a relationship to Jesse's family. Also, it appears that the first and second generations of Jesse James' descendants were somewhat reserved in admitting their relationship, while the third expresses pride in their ancestor and openly contributes family information important to the story.

Just as family researchers seek to find a genealogy connection, hundreds also seek to prove old family album photograph images are those of Jesse James. Confusing history just as much as the hundreds of fiction novels have done are the dozens of photos that have appeared over the years that are purported to be Jesse James when, in fact, they are not.

Being a wanted man with large rewards offered for your capture dead or alive would normally suppress any desire to be photographed. Such was not, however, the case with Jesse James. As this text will show, Jesse was apparently quite proud of his appearance and, after the Civil War, had photos made almost annually. Care was used to make sure copies of such photos were only given to family members who kept them carefully hidden from any lawman or newspaper reporter.

We first met at the 1981 James family reunion. Thereafter, we have served together on the board of directors of "Friends of the James Farm" and currently serve together on the "James-Younger Gang" board of directors, of which Phillip currently serves as president. We have shared our James family research and have worked closely together for more than fifteen years.

We were also close friends of Dr. William A. Settle of Tulsa, Oklahoma, who spent a lifetime researching the James-Younger story. Settle's book *Jesse James Was His Name,* published by the University of Nebraska Press, is recognized as the most accurate and complete story of the James brothers and the era represented by them in American history. We have also known and shared research with Marley Brant for many years. Her book *The Outlaw Youngers: A Confederate Brotherhood,* by Madison Books, is recognized as the best and most accurate account of the Younger brothers. We are greatly indebted for research provided by these two authors in the preparation of this material.

It is not our intent to discredit any individual or publication that disagrees with the determinations and opinions regarding accurate and nonaccurate photographs being presented here. After several years of in-depth study and application as well as the techniques used to determine photograph accuracy as explained in the following chapters, it is our intent to preserve such photographic history here. Based on these studies and Warfel's many years of training in portrait art and anatomy, we believe the Warfel portraits in the last chapter depict true images of Jesse James during various periods of his life.

Considering the fact that Jesse James obviously enjoyed having his photo taken, there may well be many other photos of him later found stored away in attic trunks. As such may surface, we hope this text will be beneficial in helping to recognize and authenticate any such photos found in the future.

PHILLIP W. STEELE
GEORGE WARFEL

The Many Faces of
JESSE JAMES

CHAPTER 1

The Life and Images of Jesse James

It was an exceptionally warm summer day in the bluegrass country of Logan County, Kentucky, when Robert Sallee James, the fifth child of John and Mary Poor James, was born on July 17, 1818. John James was a farmer and lay minister in the region who greatly admired a minister friend, Reverend Sallee. He therefore chose to honor his friend by giving Robert his middle name.

Growing up in a devoutly religious family, not only did young Robert learn to become an excellent farmer and breeder of fine Kentucky horses, but he also shared his father's interest in preaching the gospel. At age twenty-one Robert entered Georgetown College in nearby Georgetown, Kentucky. The tall, handsome, and bright Robert James soon became a campus leader. Although his course of study covered a broad area, his greatest interest was in religion. Robert graduated from Georgetown in 1843.

While attending college he met Zerelda Elizabeth Cole, the daughter of John and Sallie Lindsay Cole, at a revival meeting. Zerelda's father had been killed in a horse accident in 1827, and her mother then married Robert Thomason, a widower with six children. According to family history, Zerelda despised Thomason and, therefore, chose to stay in Kentucky under the guardianship of her uncle, James Lindsay, when the Thomasons left to settle in Clay County, Missouri.

Zerelda was attending St. Catherine's Academy, a Catholic school for girls in Lexington, when she met Robert James. Robert and Zerelda were married in her uncle's home in Stamping Ground, Kentucky, on December 28, 1841.

Robert and Zerelda soon followed the Thomasons to Missouri for a visit. Desiring to continue his seminary work in graduate school at Georgetown, Robert left Zerelda with the Thomason family and returned to Kentucky. Zerelda was pregnant with their first child at the time, and Robert had planned on returning to Missouri before the child was born. Due to a very harsh winter preventing steamboat travel on the frozen rivers, he did not make it to Missouri until after their son Alexander Franklin James was born on January 10, 1843. Shortly before their second son, Robert, was born on July 19, 1845, the Reverend James acquired a 275-acre farm near the Centerville (now Kearney, Missouri) Community. This second son only lived thirty-three days.

Jesse Woodson James was then born to the family on September 5, 1847, and Susan Lavenia on November 25, 1849. Never would they have expected that their third son, Jesse James, was destined to become a notorious outlaw and perhaps America's greatest folk hero during his short thirty-three years on this earth.

The Reverend James soon developed an excellent farm with the slaves he had brought from Kentucky and with his fine Kentucky breeding horses. He also found time to preach the gospel throughout the region and founded two churches that are still in existence in Clay County, Missouri, today. He regularly held revivals and baptism services and was extremely popular as a minister and farmer. A strong believer in education, he insisted that his children receive the best education possible. Robert James was also one of the founding members of the committee that started William Jewell College in Liberty, Missouri.

When gold was discovered in California in 1849, thousands rushed to the West Coast to seek their fortunes. A wagon train made up of Clay County residents was formed in 1850.

Since most of those going west were friends and members of Reverend James' congregation, he was encouraged to go along with the wagon train to minister to their needs.

It also had been a number of years since he had seen his brother Drury Woodson James, who had become a successful rancher and founder of a health resort in Paso Robles, California. He apparently desired to visit his brother and perhaps join him in a gold mining venture, the proceeds from which he could use to better educate his children and further develop his Baptist missionary dreams. Robert, therefore, left his wife Zerelda and three children on the Clay County farm and headed west.

Whatever dreams Robert James may have had were not to be realized, however, as shortly after his arrival in California, Robert died from some sort of stomach cramps or food poisoning on August 18, 1850, in a Placerville gold camp. He was buried there in an unmarked grave. Frank James was age seven, Jesse barely three, and Susan not quite age one at the time of their father's death.

Certainly this loss of their father at such early ages affected Frank and Jesse, who remembered him the most. Zerelda, recognizing the need for her children to have a father, then married a neighboring farmer, Benjamin Simms, a widower with several children, on September 30, 1952. This was not a successful union. The James children would not accept Simms' fatherly authority. He often beat the children, causing violent protests from Zerelda. Divorce was imminent, but Simms conveniently was killed in a horse accident before they divorced.

Robert's brother William James operated a general store in Greenville, Missouri, in which he rented space to Dr. Reuben Samuel for his family medical practice. Dr. Samuel was the son of Fielding and Mary Samuel, who settled after the Civil War near the community of Clifty in northwest Arkansas. A graduate of the Ohio Medical School, Reuben Samuel was not only a highly respected doctor in the region, but he also was a gentle and friendly man who loved children. William

James felt such a man would be perfect for Zerelda and her children and made arrangements for them to meet. As hoped, Reuben and Zerelda fell in love and were married on September 25, 1855.

The James children grew to love their stepfather, and he became the highly respected only father the James children ever knew. Zerelda and Dr. Samuel also had their own children. Sarah (Sallie) Louisa was born December 26, 1858; John Thomas, December 25, 1861; Fannie Quantrill, October 18, 1863; and Archie Peyton, July 26, 1866. Perry Samuel, whose true father remains questionable, was born to one of the family's slave women but raised by Zerelda as part of their family.

The James children grew up in a loving and highly disciplined family. They attended school, regular church services, and worked on the farm like most other farm youths of the region. This peaceful farm life was, however, interrupted by the strong antislavery sentiment that had developed throughout the bordering state of Kansas. As early as 1855, a full six years before the Civil War was to begin in 1861, abolitionist leaders such as Jim Lane, John Brown, and others were directing raids into Missouri. Justifying their raids as doing the Lord's work, such parties would steal slaves, return them to Kansas, and give them their freedom. Often farm homes, barns, and crops along this border country were burned or destroyed. The James children, therefore, grew up with an atmosphere of fear and hate surrounding their daily lives. Such childhood experiences almost surely had great influence on the personalities and attributes of not only the James brothers but also of those of all farm youths along the Missouri-Kansas border during the period.

Photography was in its infancy when the James children were growing up on their Missouri farm. It is possible that traveling family photographers occasionally traveled through the James farm region, and as most mothers, Zerelda would have wanted photos made of her children. No such James children photos have been documented in the family archives,

Jesse James' first known photograph was made at age 14 or 15 in a Kansas City studio. (Courtesy of the James family)

however. Certainly the turmoil and early winds of war that existed along this border country may have prevented such photographers from coming into the region. Such photography was also expensive, and most families of the region seldom spent money on such luxuries.

The earliest documented photograph of Jesse James appears to be a Kansas City studio photo made in 1862, shortly before Jesse would leave home to join the Quantrill guerilla forces at age fifteen. Possibly visiting some of his numerous relatives in Kansas City or attending a fair or horse race event, he chose to have his first known photo made. Jesse had not as yet developed the somewhat arrogant and often violent personality he would portray during and after the Civil War. The photo reflects his youthful innocence and, to some degree, the bitterness of growing up along the turbulent border. Soon to be a man, he is wearing what may have been his first suit, or the studio may have lent him the coat and tie for the photo because the coat appears to be a bit too large for him.

Jesse's second known photograph would not be made until 1864, shortly after Jesse officially joined Quantrill's guerilla forces at age sixteen. The James family, being slave owners, naturally supported the Confederate cause when the Civil War began in 1861.

Frank James enlisted in the Confederate army in Centerville, Missouri, on May 4, 1861, at age eighteen. Jesse, only fourteen years of age, was too young to be accepted. Although he desperately wanted to join his brother in the Confederate ranks, he necessarily remained at home.

Frank James participated in the important battle of Wilson's Creek in southwest Missouri. During action there, Frank contracted measles and, while hospitalized in nearby Springfield, Missouri, was captured by Union forces. Rather than being imprisoned, he chose to pledge his allegiance to the Union, was released, and returned home. Shortly thereafter, Frank left to join many of his farm boy friends of the region to serve in the guerilla forces under the command of William Clark Quantrill.

Quantrill was a hate-filled former Kansas schoolteacher originally from Ohio. Although not officially a part of the Confederate army or recognized by them, Quantrill's band of Missouri farm boys soon proved to be the bloodiest fighting force in the war and greatly contributed to the Confederate cause.

Still desiring to participate in fighting those who had caused so much strife and suffering throughout most of his lifetime, young Jesse remained on the farm to help the family. While plowing the fields behind his home in late May of 1863, he was suddenly surrounded by a party of mounted Federal troops who demanded that Jesse tell them the location of his brother Frank and Quantrill's camp. Because Jesse refused to give the Federal troops any information whatsoever, the raiding party finally left after severely whipping young Jesse with bullwhips and leaving him bleeding in the field. Half crawling back to the farmhouse, he found his mother Zerelda desperately trying to cut the rope from which her husband, Dr. Samuel, was left hanging.

While Jesse was being beaten in the field, another Federal party had attempted to get similar information from Dr. Samuel. After hanging him from a tree in the yard, they let him down and hanged him repeatedly as he was asked about Quantrill's camp. Refusing to answer, he was again hanged. After repeating this procedure three times, the party rode away, leaving Dr. Samuel hanging.

Dr. Samuel miraculously survived the events of the day, but the loss of oxygen to his brain caused by the hanging severely affected his mind. Consequently, he could not practice medicine or provide for his family any longer. Eventually, he required placement in a mental hospital in St. Joseph, Missouri, where he remained until his death on March 1, 1908.

No longer could Jesse James stay out of the war. This hate-filled fifteen-year-old youth left to join the guerilla ranks, where he would serve under the leadership of the treacherous "Bloody Bill" Anderson. In spite of his youth, young Jesse soon gained respect because of his horsemanship, his ability with guns, and his fearlessness as he charged into enemy ranks. Personally bringing down Union Major A. V. Johnson during the battle of Centralia on September 20, 1864, he became a battlefield hero at age seventeen.

Extremely proud to finally get to serve within the guerilla ranks, Jesse had his second known photograph made in a Platte City, Missouri, studio. Shown wearing the official guerilla shirt and hat, Jesse holds a Colt Patterson pistol in his right hand and has two others in his belt. The tie was probably provided by the street photographer. His facial expression here has noticeably changed from that of his first photograph. His pride and fearless determination are clearly revealed as the war begins to mold Jesse James.

Being an ambrotype photograph requiring a negative to be made from a glass plate then transferred to a tintype, the image is reversed, making Jesse appear here to be left-handed, which he was not. Jesse had accidently shot off the tip of his middle finger on his left hand in a gun accident before leaving the farm. Being the son of a respected Baptist minister, Jesse refused to curse and chose to shout out in pain, "Dingus!" when the accident occurred. Frank James thereafter referred to Jesse as "Dingus," as did a good many of Jesse's close friends. Frank had been given the nickname of "Buck" by his family at an early age.

Jesse was quite self-conscious of his mangled left-hand finger and is carefully concealing his left hand in this second photograph. The left-hand fingers are also carefully hidden from the camera in all of his future photographs.

Jesse proved his hero status in numerous other confrontations with Union forces. Riding in support of Col. Jo Shelby's brigade in northwest Arkansas, Jesse was with a small scouting party when they noticed that Shelby had been surrounded by Union officers and was being asked to surrender along the

This photograph of Jesse James in his guerilla uniform was made at age 16 in Platte City, Missouri. (Courtesy of the James Farm Museum)

Fayetteville-Prairie Grove road. The small group, under the leadership of Jesse James and possibly also his brother Frank, charged into the Union officers with such ferocity the Federals scattered, giving Shelby his chance to escape.

After still other heroic performances in the Battle of Cane Hill near the Indian Territory border in northwest Arkansas and the Battle of Big Cabin Creek in Indian Territory, Jesse followed a group of his guerilla friends into Texas as they realized the cause for which they had so dearly fought was rapidly being lost. There they recuperated and considered their options for the future.

Certainly embittered over losing the war and no doubt depressed over losing a way of life forever, they soon realized their only hope of returning to their farm homes and of finally having peace was to surrender. Riding with a party back to Missouri and carrying a white flag, the group rode into Lexington, Missouri, where they planned to surrender at the Federal garrison stationed there. The events that followed no doubt affected Jesse James' personality and further intensified his desire for vengeance, which molded his future direction toward a career as an outlaw. The party was suddenly fired upon by Federals as they approached the garrison. Jesse was wounded in the right lung.

The thought of seeking to obey Federal orders and surrender peaceably, then almost losing his life by trusting the Union officials for the first time—this turn of events understandably had a great affect on his life. Jesse would continue to suffer from his chest wound throughout his life. Thereafter, he was never known to surrender officially to the Union.

His mother Zerelda and stepfather Dr. Samuel, along with six other families from Clay County, had been forced to leave the county due to their Confederate sympathies. The family went to Rulo, Nebraska, where Zerelda took employment as a schoolteacher to support her husband, now a mental invalid, and the Samuel children. Jesse James went to Rulo to recuperate from his wounds. Failing to improve after several weeks, he feared death and requested he be returned to Missouri where he might be buried in Missouri soil. Zerelda took her son by steamboat down the Missouri River where they debarked in the Harlem section of North Kansas City.

Mary James, a sister of Jesse's father Robert, had married John Mimms in 1827. The Mimms were operating a boarding house in Kansas City. Fearing to return to their Clay County farm home, they were taken in by the Mimms. During his some eight weeks there, Jesse's cousin Zerelda Mimms, named after his mother, carefully nursed Jesse. Not only did her loving care result in Jesse's improvement, the two fell in love during this period, which would result in their eventual marriage. Jesse had learned of a Dr. Paul Eve of Nashville, Tennessee, who had gained a reputation for specializing in the treatment of lung wounds. He desired to go to Nashville to see Dr. Eve, but neither he nor his family had the financial means for such a trip.

Still extremely bitter over the Confederate loss of the war, the numerous Federal discriminations against those who had participated in guerilla activities during the war, and tragedies the Union had created in his life, Jesse James no doubt felt the Union owed him a great deal. Along with other former guerilla associates with similar feelings, the nation's first peacetime bank robbery was planned. Frank James, Cole and Jim Younger, and others totalling some ten men successfully robbed the Clay County Savings Association Bank in Liberty, Missouri, of approximately $72,000 on February 13, 1866. A young boy, George C. "Jolly" Wymore, was killed by crossfire in the street as the party shot their way out of the bank. Thus began what newspapers designated as the James-Younger gang.

The James family has often said that Jesse, being too weak to participate in the robbery, remained at home during the affair. Jack Wymore, owner of the Liberty Bank and Museum, has researched the event thoroughly for many years. Based on eye-witness descriptions recorded at the time, it is generally believed that Jesse James was present with the party.

Now highly wanted men, Jesse and Frank James left for

Tennessee, where they stayed with their aunt and uncle, Nancy and George Hite, in Adairsville, Kentucky, along the Tennessee border. Not only was the region a safe retreat for the James brothers, Jesse consulted with Dr. Eve and further recuperated at the Hite home for several weeks.

It was during this period in Tennessee that his third known photograph was made in 1865. This third photograph clearly reveals the poor health with which Jesse suffered. Jesse appeared to be a thin 130-35 pounds, gaunt, and stooped. His clothing was clearly all too large for him. Appearing with Jesse in the original Nashville photo were his brother Frank and a former guerilla friend, Charles F. ("Fletch") Taylor, who had lost an arm during the war. Jesse conceals his left-hand finger in his coat pocket in this photo.

It was also during this period at the Hite home that Jesse almost died from an overdose of morphine. Some past writers have indicated that this may have been a suicide attempt since Jesse was suffering badly and also depressed over his sister Susan's planning to marry Allen Parmer. There is no factual basis for this theory, however, and the James family believes the overdose was strictly accidental. A Dr. T. Simmons was brought in to treat Jesse.

Jesse's fourth photo, featuring Jesse in a business suit, was also made in Nashville in 1866. This photograph, showing Jesse still thin but apparently improving somewhat, indicates his health had prevented him from visiting a barbershop.

Jesse was advised that a change to a drier climate would be beneficial for healing his lung wound. Not able to withstand the long trip overland to California, Jesse traveled to New York, where he took a ship from New York harbor. Frank traveled overland with plans to meet Jesse in San Francisco. Jesse debarked on the eastern coast of Panama, then took a train across the isthmus to the western coast. There he took another ship to San Francisco.

Jesse's fifth known photo was made in San Francisco in 1867. Showing him immaculately dressed as a San Francisco

This photo made in Nashville, Tennessee, in 1865, shows Jesse (right) obviously thin and suffering badly from his Civil War lung wound. Charles F. ("Fletch") Taylor of Platte County, Wisconsin, who served with the James brothers in the guerilla forces, appears on the left. Jesse's brother Frank James, in a Civil War studio costume, is sitting. (Author's collection)

Jesse James, immaculately dressed in a business suit as he appeared in Nashville, Tennessee, in 1866. (Author's collection)

Jesse James in a San Francisco photo gallery in 1867. (Courtesy of the James family)

businessman, the photo indicates his health has further improved. Again, his left-hand fingers are carefully curled out of camera view.

While in California, Jesse and Frank looked for, unsuccessfully, the grave of their father, who had died in Placerville, California, in 1850. They then visited their uncle, Drury Woodson James, who had become a very successful cattle rancher there. Drury had also founded a health resort around the mineral springs of Paso Robles, California. Not only did the California climate prove to greatly help Jesse, his many baths in the Paso Robles mineral waters also contributed to his recovery.

Apparently returning overland after several weeks of visiting their California relative, Jesse and Frank James found conditions in Missouri to be no longer safe for them. Not only were large rewards being offered for those who participated in the Liberty Bank robbery in which young Wymore was killed, their friend John Newman Edwards of the *Kansas City Times* newspaper had helped create their folk hero image through his regular editorials. Edwards had served in the Confederate army with Col. Jo Shelby and, being sympathetic of the atrocities former guerilla forces were now being subjected to, regularly justified the actions of the James-Younger gang through his romantic editorials.

Such articles created the legend of Jesse James and depicted him as a master bandit, who moved quickly around the nation and made a fool out of lawmen. While the James brothers had been peaceably living in Tennessee and California, they were being blamed, along with their friends, the Younger brothers, for almost every robbery in the nation. They were no doubt surprised to learn when they returned from California that in addition to the Liberty Bank robbery, they were also being sought for the robbery of the Mitchell and Company banking firm of Lexington, Missouri, on October 30, 1866. It is possible that they did participate in the Lexington robbery, but most students of James-Younger gang history feel that the James brothers left

Missouri for Tennessee shortly after the Liberty robbery in February of 1866.

Their funds were now depleted from their months of travel and, no doubt, a few heavy gambling losses because of their frequency at horse racing events around the Nashville region. Since they were being accused of numerous robberies around the nation and were wanted men, they must have decided that they might as well continue such activities. After all, the admiring public John Newman Edward's editorials and a few dime novel fiction writers had created expected nothing less. The thriving border city of Russellville, Kentucky, was therefore to be their next target. On March 20, 1868, the gang robbed the Southern Deposit Bank in Russellville of $14,000.

It is believed the James brothers spent the remainder of 1868 and most of 1869 in the Nashville region. Jesse assumed the name of John Davis Howard and Frank, Ben Woodson for their Tennessee aliases, both names being taken from their Howard and Woodson family ancestors. Posing as grain buyers and horse dealers, the James brothers supported themselves by both racing and gambling around the many tracks in the Nashville and Kentucky regions. Sometime in 1869, they again returned to Missouri, no doubt wanting to see their family and to renew the courtships Jesse was having with his cousin Zee Mimms and brother Frank with Annie Ralston.

Continuing their love for horses and racing events, the James brothers traveled to such events around western Kansas, Iowa, and Illinois. It is believed that during one such event around Greenville, Illinois, Jesse's sixth known photograph was taken. Appearing to be much healthier and now somewhat proud of the fact that he was a frequent subject in newspaper and dime novel publications, he begins to display his egotistical, fun-loving, devil-may-care nonchalance.

Apparently once again needing a bank roll, the James brothers, along with their associates, the Younger brothers, and other proven gang members, selected the Davies County Savings Bank of Gallatin, Missouri, from which they hoped to

Jesse James in Greenville, Illinois, in 1869. (Courtesy of the James family)

gain needed cash. This robbery proved to be disastrous for the gang. Being sons of a respected Baptist minister, they could justify taking funds from federally owned and controlled institutions, but killing, unless in self-defense, was strictly forbidden for the gang Jesse usually controlled. Not only did the Gallatin robbery produce only a meager $700 in cash, but cashier John W. Sheets was killed. Now their arrest warrants were for murder as well as bank robbery, which fully established a point of no return for the notorious James brothers and their associates.

Although the James and Younger brothers were being blamed for almost any criminal activity in the nation, their next robbery would not be until some seventeen months later. Other than continuing their travels around to Missouri, Kansas, Iowa, Tennessee, and Kentucky racetracks, little is known of their activities in 1870 and 1871. Sometime in 1871, the James brothers traveled to Long Branch, New Jersey. It was most likely soon after the gang robbed the Ocobock Brothers Bank in Corydon, Iowa, of some $6,000 on June 3, 1871.

Long Branch was a famous resort along the New Jersey coast that offered numerous gambling opportunities with both cards and horses, as well as fun and relaxation. Jesse, who continued to experience pain from his war wounds, undoubtably enjoyed the warm summer beach. In Long Branch his seventh known studio photograph was made. His appearance as a well-dressed riverboat gambler holding a studio cane reveals the same pride and somewhat arrogant expression of his Illinois photo two years earlier. The violence characterizing his years of carefully avoiding capture and experience as a bank robber now begin to be reflected in his eyes and expression. Carefully exposing only the fingers on his right hand, he again conceals his mangled left-hand middle finger.

Almost one year after the Corydon robbery, the gang was credited with the robbery of the bank in Columbia, Kentucky, on April 29, 1872. Cashier R. A. C. Martin lost his life during

Jesse James in a Long Branch, New Jersey, studio in 1871. (Courtesy of the James family)

his ill-fated attempt to save his deposits. Some $6,000 was taken in the robbery.

Five months later, the James brothers were back in Missouri. Realizing the large amounts of cash on hand at the Kansas City Fair offices and knowing a raid of this type presented far less risk than their past raids on banks, the James brothers robbed the fair cashier of $8,000 on September 26, 1872. Jesse James' eighth known photograph, which was found in the family of Jo Ann Byland of Carrollton, Illinois, in 1990, was made. Frank James appears in the photo with Jesse in what is believed to have been made by a street photographer during one of their visits to a fair or horse race in the region. Jesse's proud and egotistical arrogance again is depicted in his face. The photo has been reversed during duplication from the original tintype and again reveals careful disguise of his left-hand middle finger by curling it around his lapel.

May 27, 1873, the James-Younger gang struck the St. Genevieve, Missouri, Savings Association, resulting in $4,000 for the robbers. They were hoping to obtain a much larger amount from a payroll deposit there, but it had been transferred to St. Louis the day before. Six weeks later, on July 21, 1873, the James-Younger gang's first train robbery proved to be the most successful in their career. Knowing the small gains they had realized from most of their bank robberies were not worth the risks, they executed their bold plan to rob the Chicago, Rock Island, and Pacific train near Adair, Iowa. Engineer John Rafferty was killed, and $26,000 was obtained from the express car and passengers.

One of the rarest known documented photos of Jesse James is also believed to have been made in 1873. This ninth photo was made by a studio photographer in Clarinda, Iowa. While attending horse race events in Iowa, Jesse had this photo taken while plans for their Adair train robbery were being made. This image was accidentally found among a box of photos Erich Bauman purchased in a northern California

Jesse James, left, with his brother Frank in Illinois in 1872.
(Courtesy of Jo Ann Byland)

Jesse James, Clarinda, Iowa, 1873. (Courtesy of Erich Bauman)

junk shop. Coming from the estate sale of an O. H. Park, it can only be assumed that the Park family was somehow connected to the Iowa photographer who originally made this photograph of Jesse.

Apparently Jesse and Frank James and their Younger associates drifted south after the Adair robbery. Hot Springs, Arkansas, was a popular resort, and Jesse, still suffering pain from his war wounds, no doubt found the mineral baths offered in Arkansas helpful. Noting the wealthy tourists from major Northern cities frequenting Hot Springs, the gang's first known stagecoach robbery was planned. Visitors to Hot Springs came by train to Malvern, Arkansas, where they were met by stagecoaches for the fifty-mile trip to the resort city. On January 15, 1874, a party believed to have been led by Jesse James stopped such a coach and relieved the passengers of their cash and jewelry. Reports of the final count taken vary from $1,000 to $8,000. Certainty of Jesse James' being with the party would later be confirmed upon his death. Among Jesse's effects was found a gold pocket watch that had been taken from one of the passengers.

Two weeks after the Hot Springs robbery, the gang held up the St. Louis Iron Mountain and Southern Railroad train at Gads Hill, Missouri, on January 31, 1874. Although much less than their first train robbery netted, the $10,000 taken exceeded most of their bank robbery amounts.

A tenth photo of Jesse James has been documented for the 1874 period. As he would have appeared in 1874 during both the Hot Springs and Gads Hill robberies, he probably had this photo made in a Hot Springs studio. Jesse's normal businessman attire in most previous photographs did not fit the notorious and illusive outlaw and gunfighter image so many dime novel fiction writers had created. Jesse appears here to be jestfully dressing with a western hat, bandanna, gunbelt, and rifle, the way his loyal readers would expect him to appear. Most likely the hat, gunbelt, and rifle were props of a studio photographer. Again, his left hand is carefully concealed.

Jesse James, 1874. Photo is believed to have been made in a Hot Springs, Arkansas, studio. (Courtesy of the James family)

Jesse's long love affair and periodic courtship of Zee Mimms had gone on since 1866. Finally, Jesse may have realized that his life on the run, constantly in fear of being shot down by the numerous bounty hunters seeking rewards, was not the life he had dreamed of having. Hoping to retire from the outlaw life and having now mellowed from the revenge he had harbored from war days, he felt it was time to get married, settle down, and become a peaceful farmer. No doubt the beautiful Zee Mimms also made such demands for his lifestyle to change before accepting his proposal. On April 24, 1874, Jesse James and Zee Mimms were married in the home of Lucy Browder, a sister to Zee, in Centerville (now Kearney), Missouri. Although William James, Jesse's uncle, tried to convince Zee that it would be foolish to marry his outlaw nephew, he did perform the ceremony.

Jesse and Zee chose to honeymoon in Texas. Legend tells of their spending a few days in the Roaring River State Park resort area in Missouri as they traveled south. Jesse's sister Susan had married Allen Parmer on November 24, 1870, and moved to the Cane Hill, Arkansas, region to live on the Parmer family farm there. Susan taught school in the nearby Bethesda Community. Apparently tiring of farm labor, Allen Parmer decided to move with Susan to Texas, where opportunity for employment in railroad construction could be found. Sometime before the marriage of Jesse and Zee, the Parmers had moved to Sherman, Texas, where Susan once again taught school. Jesse and Zee spent several weeks with the Parmers during their wedding trip.

An Austin and San Antonio, Texas, stagecoach was robbed and plundered on April 7, 1874. Again, the James-Younger gang were suspected, but considering the logistics and time required for travel, it is most doubtful either of the James brothers was present at the Austin-San Antonio stage robbery. Since Jesse was to marry on April 24 in Missouri, it is doubtful he would have left Texas on April 8, gotten married April 24, and returned to Texas on his honeymoon. Frank James is believed to have been in Virginia and Nebraska between January and June of 1874. Frank married Annie Ralston in Omaha, Nebraska, in June of 1874.

Cole Younger, his brothers Bob and Jim, and Jim Reed, another former guerilla associate who had married Belle Shirley in Collin County, Texas, in 1866, very well could have been in the party that robbed the Austin-San Antonio stage. The Youngers had moved their mother to the safety of Texas during the Civil War. Numerous other families from western Missouri as well as many former Quantrill followers had gone to Texas after the war. Belle Shirley (Myra Maebelle Shirley), who later became the notorious Belle Starr after Jim Reed was killed by a bounty hunter in 1875, had a close relationship with the Youngers during this period in Texas.

The eleventh photo of Jesse James is believed to have been made during this period. It is the only known photo of Jesse on horseback. Legend within the James family indicates that this is a photo of Jesse on his favorite horse, "Stonewall," who was named after Stonewall Jackson. The family story tells that this photo was made in Sherman, Texas, during his visit with Susan while on his honeymoon.

The incident that firmly placed the James brothers in the realm of folk heroes and created national public sympathy for the outlaws occurred on the night of January 26, 1875. Allen Pinkerton, Chief of the Pinkerton Detective Agency and founder of the U. S. Secret Service, had been employed to bring down the notorious James-Younger gang. The fact that the gang had continued to plunder banks and trains for several years was an embarrassment for the Pinkerton Agency. Although the James brothers were miles away from their James-Samuel family farm, the Pinkertons had reason to believe they were there. Shortly after midnight, their posse surrounded the cabin, and a bomb device was thrown through a bedroom window. Hearing the noise, Mrs. Samuel ran into the room and attempted to shove the device into the fireplace. As she did, the bomb exploded. Shrapnel from

The only known photograph of Jesse James on horseback; he is shown here on his favorite horse "Stonewall." The photo is believed to have been made in Sherman, Texas, while Jesse and Zee were honeymooning in 1874. (Courtesy of James R. Ross, great-grandson of Jesse James)

the explosion struck eight-year-old Archie Peyton Samuel, Jesse and Frank James' stepbrother, and killed him. Mrs. Samuel's right arm was mangled so badly in the explosion it required amputation at the elbow.

Strongly criticized by the public for their attack on an innocent family, the Pinkertons explained that the event was an accident. According to their reports at the time, the device was actually a flare they hoped to use to light up the home to see if the James boys were in the house. It was their contention that the device would not have exploded if Mrs.

Samuel had not shoved it into the fireplace. James researchers Ted Yeatman of Maryland and Fred Egloff of Chicago discovered letters in the Library of Congress and the Pinkerton Archives in 1992 that prove conclusively that the device was definitely a bomb obtained from the Rock Island, Illinois, Arsenal in December of 1874, and plans had indeed been made to destroy the James-Samuel home.

Returning to Missouri, Jesse apparently left Zee with her parents in Kansas City while he traveled to Nebraska in search of a farm or business venture to settle into. While in Nebraska City, Nebraska, his most famous and most often published photo was taken in 1875. Because he was neatly dressed and finely groomed, few would have guessed him to be the notorious robber of banks, trains, and coaches. Both this photo and the next one, which was worn in a locket by Jesse's mother, Zerelda Samuel, are commonly believed to have been made during this visit to Nebraska. However, it is possible that the locket photo was made during Jesse's time in Long Branch.

The gang's next robbery may have been motivated by their finding many Nebraska farm properties appealing. Perhaps one more robbery could generate the funds required for Jesse's retirement from his outlaw career. Far from the Midwest territory lawmen most expected the James-Younger gang to appear in next, Jesse chose to take Zee along with him to Tennessee, where on August 31, 1875, the couple's first child, Jesse Edwards James, was born. Jesse chose to honor John Newman Edwards, the Kansas City journalist who continued to treat the James and Younger brothers kindly through his romantic editorials, by so naming his first child.

Although it seems most unreasonable for Jesse James to have left his wife and newborn son to participate in robbing the bank of Huntington, West Virginia, only six days after his son's birth, the September 6, 1875, robbery was credited to the James-Younger gang. They took $20,000 in the robbery.

The gang returned to Missouri in July of 1876, where a

The most famous photo of Jesse James was made in Nebraska City, Nebraska, in 1875. (Courtesy of the James family)

A locket picture Jesse had made in Nebraska City, Nebraska, or possibly Long Branch, New Jersey, for his mother Zerelda. (Courtesy of the James family)

Missouri-Pacific train was robbed of $17,000 on July 7. Leasing a farm near Waverly, Tennessee, they planned the robbery that ultimately brought an end to the James-Younger association. Again, far from familiar territory, the gang traveled to Minnesota, where they rode into the community of Northfield and attempted to rob the First National Bank on September 7, 1876. Not expecting to be met with such defense by the citizens there, two members of the gang, Charley Pitts and Bill Chadwell, were killed. Cole, Jim, and Bob Younger were shot to pieces and captured by a posse two weeks later. The Younger brothers survived their wounds and were given life sentences in the Minnesota State Prison in Stillwater. Although Jesse James received a bullet wound in the thigh and Frank in the leg, they somehow escaped and returned to Tennessee.

Twin boys, Gould and Montgomery—named after two doctors of the region, Dr. Jay Gould and Dr. Montgomery—were born to Jesse and Zee soon after Jesse's return from the ill-fated Minnesota disaster. These twin boys only lived a few days and were buried on their Waverly, Tennessee, farm.

Finding it difficult to earn a living farming in Waverly and running up large debts in the region, Jesse moved his family into Nashville. For several weeks Jesse, Zee, and Jesse Edwards—as John Davis, Zee, and Tim Howard—stayed with Frank and Annie James and their young son, Robert James, who had been born to them on February 6, 1878. Jesse later moved his family to a nice brick home on Fatherland Street in the exclusive Edgehill district of Nashville. This may have been after the James gang successfully took $40,000 in the robbery of the Chicago, Alton, and St. Louis train at Glendale, Missouri, on October 8, 1879.

Samuel family tradition in northwest Arkansas tells of their James relatives often taking refuge at Fielding Samuel's remote Arkansas Ozarks farm near the Clifty community. Fielding was the father of Dr. Reuben Samuel, who was the stepfather of Frank, Jesse, and Susan James. Perhaps the James

According to the Samuel Family of Arkansas, Frank and Jesse James, in hats, appear here on the porch of the Samuel home near Clifty, Arkansas. Fielding and Mary Samuel, parents of the James brothers' stepfather, Dr. Reuben Samuel, appear on the lawn with other family members. Jesse James cannot be fully authenticated in this photo; only family tradition substantiates. (Courtesy of Clifford Samuel, Springdale, Arkansas)

brothers visited their Arkansas relatives after the Glendale robbery. Appearing dressed as cowboys or farm hands on the front porch in a Samuel family photo from the 1880 period, they most likely avoided the suspicion their normal business-suit attire might have caused. Due to the poor quality and nature of this photograph, documentation of its accuracy must rely on the fact that it has been told over the years within this family that the two men in hats on the porch are Frank and Jesse.

What would be the fifteenth photo of Jesse James from the 1880 period surfaced in 1992 within the family of James A. Tapp in Oklahoma. Tapp's family descends from Lewis

This rare photograph of Jesse James surfaced in the Tapp family of Ponca City, Oklahoma, in 1994. Included in a box of old photographs given to James A. Tapp by his grandmother was this group photo. Since the Tapp family settled on a farm next to the James family in Clay County, Missouri, in 1852, this photo was sent to George Warfel for inspection. Mr. Warfel was able to determine that the well-dressed gentleman standing in the center was none other than Jesse James. At this time, the others in the photo have not been identified. This is the only known photo of Jesse with his hair parted in the middle; the boy standing to his right seems to be imitating his style and may be John Samuel, Jesse's half-brother. It is believed to have been taken around 1877. (Courtesy of James A. Tapp)

Washington and Mary Ellen Hickman Tapp, whose farm in Clay County, Missouri, adjoined the James-Samuel farm. Family tradition tells of the James brothers being good friends with their Tapp family neighbors. Appearing with Tapp family members in the photo, Jesse James appears immaculately dressed. The fact that his hair is for the first time parted in the middle further confirms Jesse's concern for his appearance and the style of the period.

Also in 1880, the James gang performed their second robbery of a stagecoach. The Glasgow coach was held up and robbed on its trip between Mammoth Cave and Cave City in Edmundson County, Kentucky.

While Jesse posed as a horse and grain dealer, what funds he received from various robberies were not sufficient with which to support his family, gambling, and horse racing enterprises. Both Jesse and Frank found it necessary to take employment wherever possible. While he was employed by a cedar bucket manufacturing plant, Jesse's sixteenth documented photograph was taken. The photo was in possession of a St. Louis lady when it was brought to the attention of the late Milton F. Perry while he was serving as Superintendent of Clay County Historic Sites. Perry forwarded a copy of this photo to George Warfel in hopes Frank James' photo with a group of employees could be confirmed. While he was studying other gentlemen in the picture, he discovered what may have been the last photo of Jesse James alive within this group portrait. This picture is believed to have been made in 1880.

* * * *

A government paymaster, Alexander G. Smith, was robbed of some $5,200 shortly after leaving the bank in Muscle Shoals, Alabama, on his way to pay a construction crew on March 11, 1881. Frank James, Jesse James, and former Missouri associates Bill Ryan and Dick Liddil were with the party.

July 15, 1881, found the James brothers leading the gang that robbed the Chicago, Rock Island, and Pacific train near

Jesse James appears, fifth from the left, sitting, in a group of employees at a Nashville, Tennessee, cedar bucket factory in 1880. Frank James also appears, fourth from the right, standing, on the back row. This is believed to be the last photo of Jesse James alive. (Courtesy of Irene Knight and the James Farm Museum)

Winston, Missouri. Proving to be another unfortunate robbery—only $2,000 was taken—Conductor Westfall along with Frank McMillen, a railroad employee, were killed.

The gang's last train robbery was on September 7, 1881, at Blue Cut, near Glendale, Missouri. There some $3,000 in cash and jewelry were taken from the express car and passengers.

CHAPTER 2

The Death of Jesse James

A heavy rain storm was occurring on the night of March 25, 1881, when Bill Ryan, a James-Younger gang associate, stopped by the W. R. Maddux store and saloon in White's Creek, Tennessee, to take shelter from the storm. Ryan began drinking heartily and soon became drunk and disorderly as he threatened several others with his revolvers. Davis County Constable W. E. Earthman, who owned the Maddux store and saloon properties, was called in and, with the help of a Mr. McGinnis, soon overpowered, disarmed, and arrested Ryan. Ryan was then tied to a chair, placed in the back of a wagon, and hauled to the Nashville jail only a few miles south of White's Creek.

The next day, another James-Younger gang associate, Dick Liddil, noticed an article in the *Nashville Banner* regarding Ryan's arrest and quickly informed Frank and Jesse James, who were living in Nashville under their aliases of Ben Woodson and John Davis Howard. Ryan had been with the gang when they robbed the bank in Gallatin, Missouri; the stagecoach at Mammoth Cave, Kentucky; and the federal payroll officer near Muscle Shoals, Alabama. Not trusting Ryan, who knew well the identities of Jesse and Frank James in Nashville, Jesse and Frank soon met and decided to leave Nashville quickly. Frank chose to take his wife, Annie, and young son,

Robert, to the Roanoke and Lynchburg, Virginia, region. Jesse returned to the home of his in-laws, the Mimms family in Kansas City, along with his wife, Zee, and children, Jesse Edwards and Mary Susan, who was born in Nashville, June 17, 1879. A few months later, Jesse took his family to St. Joseph, Missouri, where he rented a home on Lafayette Street under the name of Tom Howard on Christmas Eve of 1881.

Jesse, as well as his wife, Zee, had by this time grown extremely tired of not being able to live a normal life and of living in constant fear of being found by a bounty hunter seeking the now some $10,000 for his capture—for his arrest and conviction. Then thirty-four years of age, Jesse dreamed of ending his some sixteen-year career as an outlaw and settling down on a farm where he could raise his children in peace.

Jesse had family ties in Nebraska, and both he and Frank James had used various Nebraska locations as safe retreats over the years. Jesse's uncle (for whom he was named), Jesse Cole, and other relations were in the Nebraska region. Jesse therefore took special interest in the following advertisement he saw in the *Lincoln Journal* newspaper.

> FOR SALE: A very fine 160 acres, adjoining the town of Franklin, Franklin Co. Corners with depot grounds. Living spring; beautiful creek runs through it. 90 acres in body of finest bottom land; balance natural young timber. Mill within a mile. Has good educational, religious, railroad and other facilities as any point in western Nebraska. $10 per acre. Address or call on J. D. Calhoun, Lincoln, Neb.

J. D. Calhoun was the night editor of the *Lincoln Journal* and owned a farm adjacent to the 160 acres he offered in this ad. Jesse immediately responded to the ad with the following letter:

> Mr. J. D. Calhoun
> Lincoln, Neb.
>
> Dear Sir:
>
> I have noticed that you have 160 acres for sale in Franklin

County, Neb. Please write to me at once, and let me know the lowest cash price that will buy your land. Give me a full description of the land, etc.

I want to purchase a farm of that size, provided I can find one to suit. I will not buy a farm unless the soil is No. 1.

I will start on a trip in about eight days to Northern Nebraska & Southern Nebraska, and if the description of your land suits me I will buy it. From the advertisement in the *Lincoln Journal,* I suppose your land can be made a good farm for stock and grain.

Please answer me at once.

> Respectfully,
> Tho. Howard,
> No. 1318
> Lafayette St.
> St. Joseph, Mo.

Calhoun answered Jesse's inquiry and made plans to take him to see the property. Research by Emmett Hoctor of Plattsmouth, Nebraska, and *The Rise and Fall of Jesse James* by Robertus Love, G. P. Putnam and Sons, 1926, indicates that Jesse took Charley Ford with him to Nebraska on this trip.

Jesse's funds by this time were depleted. Not only had it been many months since a robbery had been held, but Jesse's horse dealing and race betting endeavors had also not been successful. He therefore needed to pull one more robbery to finance his dream of finally retiring to a Nebraska farm.

He selected the Platte City Bank—located near where the Kansas City Airport is today—as his final conquest. Most of the former associates of the James-Younger gang were by this time either dead, in prison, or retired from their outlaw careers. Jesse was undoubtably concerned over calling on inexperienced Bob and Charley Ford to assist in the plan, but he had little choice. While staying in Jesse's home to discuss plans for the robbery, Bob Ford found the opportunity to fulfill the plot he had made with Missouri governor Thomas Crittenden and Clay County authorities to bring down, once and for all, the legendary Jesse James on the morning of April 3, 1882.

Jesse had plans for Bob and Charley Ford to ride with him that evening to Platte City to survey the area and to make final plans for the bank robbery on the morning of April 4 and their subsequent escape route. It was a beautiful Monday spring morning, and all had risen around 7 A.M. Jesse's wife Zee was not feeling well that morning, and Jesse asked Bob Ford to help Zee in the kitchen while Jesse and Charley Ford went to the stables behind the house to feed and curry their horses.

Tension had prevailed throughout the time the Fords had been staying in Jesse's home. Dick Liddil, who was a close friend of Bob Ford and a former associate of the James-Younger gang, had recently surrendered to law authorities. Because the Fords had chosen not to mention this, they feared what Jesse might do if he learned of it.

At approximately 7:45 A.M., Jesse and Charley returned to the house. While Charley helped Zee finish preparing breakfast, Bob Ford joined Jesse for a walk to a newsstand a few blocks away for the morning newspaper. Returning to the house, Jesse sat down in the parlor to scan the news. Noticeably startled when Bob Ford saw the article about Liddil's surrender and offer to help authorities apprehend Jesse James, Ford quickly tossed that section onto a chair and covered it with a shawl in hopes Jesse would overlook it. As Zee called them to breakfast, however, Jesse picked up all of the newspaper before going to the kitchen.

Obviously apprehensive about what Jesse might do, Bob Ford moved his gun to the front of his gun belt before sitting at the table directly opposite Jesse. As Zee began pouring coffee, Jesse laid the paper out on the kitchen table and immediately noticed the Liddil article. "What's this, Dick Liddil surrenders?" Jesse excitedly proclaimed. "Why didn't you boys tell me about this?" he further questioned. Unquestionably very nervous, the Fords answered the only way they could—and continue living—by explaining they didn't know about it. Because Jesse continued to question the Fords about the matter, Bob could eat no more, arose, and walked into the parlor. Charley remained at the table and continued to make excuses to substantiate their story. Jesse then arose and, with the newspaper in his hand, walked in to join Bob in the parlor. To Bob's amazement, Jesse smiled as he entered the room and assured Bob that all was well and stated that he had been too hasty in his judgment at the breakfast table.

Commenting about how warm it was, Jesse walked to the front door and opened it to let the fresh spring air into the stuffy parlor. He raised the normally always drawn window blind, then removed his coat and vest and laid them across a daybed in the corner of the room near the window. Jesse's next action has created more debate among James scholars than any other single event in his lifetime. Removing his gun belt, he laid it across the daybed next to his coat and explained that he might be seen by a passerby from the street.

Never before had Jesse James ever been known to remove his gun belt when anyone other than family members were present. Certainly the Ford brothers could not be considered good friends of Jesse's, and he had no reason to fully trust them. Some past James historians have surmised that Jesse became suspicious during their confrontation over breakfast and may have decided to test their loyalty by removing his gun belt.

Jesse then sat down on the daybed and once again began reading the newspaper. Looking up, Jesse noticed pictures in a wall grouping were extremely dusty, and the top picture, a needlepoint Jesse's mother had made and given him and Zee as a wedding present, was crooked. Members of the James family have indicated that a picture of Jesse's favorite horse, "Stonewall," was also in the grouping. As Charley Ford walked out to the front yard and Bob sat in a chair, Jesse arose, picked up a feather duster from a nearby table with his right hand, and at the same time, scooted a cane chair below the picture grouping with his left hand. The moment Jesse stood on the chair and reached for the needlepoint, Bob recognized his opportunity. As Ford pulled and cocked his gun, Jesse turned his head slightly to the right. The bullet struck Jesse just below the right ear and lodged in the frontal bone near his left ear. Jesse James was dead at approximately 8:27 A.M. The force from Ford's Colt .45,[1] single-action revolver, from such a short distance away slammed Jesse's body into the wall, off which it bounced to the floor. Falling face down, his body bounced over onto its back. The impact from hitting the wall, door molding, or floor created a deep cut and bruise on Jesse's left temple. This cut and bruise have mistakenly been referred to by some past writers as being caused by the bullet exiting the skull.

Jesse's two children and their small dog were the first to reach the parlor after hearing the shot. Zee, who was cleaning the kitchen, then rushed into the room and, kneeling over her dead husband's body, attempted to stop the blood rushing from Jesse's head. Seeing the Fords out on the lawn, Zee screamed, "Bob Ford, what have you done? Come back!" As Bob vaulted the fence, Charley walked back to the door and attempted to explain away the event as being a gun accident. The Fords then rushed toward Marshal Enos Craig's office where they hoped to surrender and tell the world they had killed Jesse James.

The brothers were not to find the authorities, however, until they returned to the scene of their crime. Sheriff Timberlake and St. Joseph Marshal Enos Craig and Marshal Finley reached the James home before the Fords returned. Zee insisted that her dead husband was Tom Howard until the

---

[1]Bob Ford stated to news reporters on May 5, 1882, that he used a Colt .45, single-action revolver, Serial Number 50432, to kill Jesse James.

Ford brothers returned to the house and she realized that the Fords' actions resulted from a plot with authorities.

A hearse from Sidenfaden's Funeral Parlor arrived to pick up Jesse's body. J. W. Graham, a young photographer with Smith's Studio, asked his employer's permission to photograph Jesse's remains. He then arrived at Sidenfaden's around 11 A.M. and received permission from authorities there to make the last photographs of Jesse James.

A coroner's inquest held at the St. Joseph Courthouse met from 4 P.M. to 6 P.M., before adjourning until 10 A.M. the next morning, April 4. Zee James, the Fords, Coroner Heddens, and others established the events of the day. Zee had sent a telegram to Jesse's mother Zerelda, and she arrived late that evening by train. At 10 P.M. an autopsy of Jesse's body was made by the coroner, Dr. J. W. Heddens; Dr. Jacob Geiger, a professor of operatic surgery in the College of Physicians; Dr. F. C. Hoyt, a professor of anatomy at the same institution; and Dr. George C. Catlett, superintendent of the State Insane Asylum there. Coroner Heddens stated that the fatal bullet was removed from Jesse's skull.

Zerelda, along with Zee James, Sheriff Timberlake, family members, and others who had known Jesse all confirmed without any doubt whatsoever that the corpse was that of Jesse Woodson James.

The Coroner's jury reviewed all of the statements made by those who performed the autopsy and those who identified the corpse. After a half-hour deliberation the following verdict was given on Tuesday morning, April 4:

> We the jury, summoned to hear the testimony in the case before us, do hereby declare that the body of the deceased is that of Jesse W. James, and that he came by his death by a wound in the back of his head caused by a pistol shot fired intentionally by the hand of Robert Ford.

On the night of April 5, Zee James, Zerelda Samuel, Zee's children, and other family members accompanied Jesse's

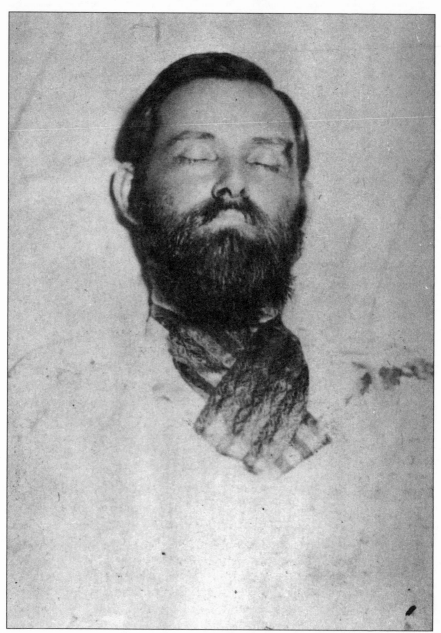

Jesse James in death by photographer R. Uhlman in St. Joseph, Missouri, 1882. (Courtesy of the James Farm Museum)

body to Kearney by train. They arrived around 2:45 A.M. Jesse's body was put on public display at the Kearney House for several hours. Hundreds passed by to gaze at the remains of America's greatest outlaw. Many were old guerilla comrades.

Jesse James' body, packed in ice, while on public display at Sidenfaden's Funeral Parlor in St. Joseph. Marshall Enos Craig, center, with two deputies guard the corpse. Scars from Jesse's wounds in the right chest are clearly visible. (Courtesy of the James Farm Museum)

Here again, none of those who had known Jesse in life had any question about the corpse being that of the Jesse James they had known.

The corpse was placed in a wagon and taken across town to the First Baptist Church for services. The services began with the hymn, "What a Friend We Have in Jesus." Rev. R. H. Jones of Lathrop, Missouri, read a passage of Scripture. The church pastor, J. M. P. Martin, preached the sermon.

The pallbearers were J. D. Ford, Charles Scott, James Henderson, J. T. Reed, and William Bond. A sixth pallbearer, which no one seemed to know, was "Jim Vaughn." One of Quantrill's men, the real Jim Vaughn was found in a barbershop in Lawrence, Kansas, during the war and hung on the street by Kansas abolitionists. Guerrillas thereafter sometimes left notes on their victims' bodies: "Remember Jim Vaughn." The demise of Jim Vaughn further prompted Quantrill's decision to burn Lawrence on August 21, 1863. The "Jim Vaughn" pallbearer was therefore representing the cause for which Jesse James and Quantrill's many followers had supported. The true identity of that sixth pallbearer still remains a mystery.

At the close of the service, the church pastor requested that only the family members accompany the party to the burial site on the Samuel farm. Some fifty buggies and wagons, however, followed the procession to the farm. Jesse's mother; wife Zee; their two children; Luther James; Fannie Quantrill Hall; Zee's mother, Mary Mimms; James relatives, Mr. and Mrs Kirkpatrick; and a few other James and Samuel family members were with the party.

Jesse's half-brother John Samuel, who had so greatly admired Jesse, was suffering from both a wound and extreme shock over the loss of Jesse and could not attend the funeral. The coffin was taken into the Samuel home upon arrival at the farm and opened near John's bedside for his last view of his beloved half-brother. Zerelda held her one arm aloft as the casket was opened and exclaimed in a loud

Zee James, wife of Jesse, with her two children, Jesse Edwards and Mary Susan, on the day of Jesse James' funeral in Kearney, Missouri. Mary Susan wears a traditional black waist band depicting their mourning in the photo. (Courtesy of the James family)

voice, "Johnny, my boy, look upon your brother Jesse. Your murdered brother Jesse!"

A short time later, the coffin was placed in a grave that had been dug in the yard only a few yards from the Samuel house. There Zerelda, fearing grave robbers and curious intruders, could watch over her famous son's grave.

As Zerelda Samuel's health deteriorated after Dr. Samuel had been placed in the St. Joseph Mental Institution, Mrs. Samuel left the farm and rented a home in Kearney. Although she had rented out the farm, she realized Jesse's grave could no longer be protected properly. Souvenir hunters had begun to chip away pieces of Jesse's grave marker and she feared further desecration of his resting place. She then had his body disinterred and moved to the Mt. Olivet Cemetery in Kearney on July 29, 1902, where Jesse's remains were reburied next to those of Zee, who had died on November 13, 1900.

Jesse's son Jesse Edwards James, a Kansas City attorney at the time, was on hand to observe the disinterrment of his father. He picked up Jesse's skull as it was uncovered and carefully examined it. The bullet hole behind the right ear was clearly noticeable but no exit hole could be found, which further proved the testimony given by the autopsy party that the bullet was removed from where it lodged in Jesse's left temple. The famous bullet was kept in the family of Coroner Heddens. A grandson of Heddens proudly displayed the bullet in its shadowbox frame in his Pasadena, California, home until it was stolen in a burglary.

The fact that Ford waited until Jesse was unarmed and shot him in the back of the head no doubt contributed more to the creation of the legend of Jesse James than any other event in his life. Numerous theories as to why Jesse would have removed his guns, turned his back to the Fords, stood on a chair, and chosen to dust and straighten a picture have been debated for more than one hundred years and will continue to be a topic of discussion. We must wonder what history

Zerelda James Samuel, mother of Jesse James, on the day of her son's funeral. Her right arm, which was amputated at the elbow after the Pinkerton bomb was thrown into her home, is clearly visible. Also note she wears a black mourning band around her left hand, which was a custom of the period. (Courtesy of the James family)

might have revealed had Jesse been successful in the performance of his last robbery, acquired the Nebraska farm, and retired to a peaceful farm life. Had this happened, we lovers of the romantic history of the James-Younger era may have been pursuing other interests.

CHAPTER 3

Image Identification
Techniques

Over the many years since Jesse James was assassinated by
Robert Newton Ford, it has become quite popular for families to seek to find a relationship to this noted bandit. The
family of William James, who originally came to America from
England and from which Jesse Woodson James descended,
has been fully documented and published. Those families
who cannot find a direct relationship with the James family
seek to find ties to those families related to Jesse through
marriage. The Mimms, Cole, Thomason, Lindsay, Howard,
Hite, Samuel, and other families offer relationship opportunities regardless of how miniscule a connection to Jesse James
might be.

This driving force within families to prove such relation-
ships to Jesse will most likely continue for many years to come,
and such family research is important and encouraged for several reasons. Jesse James and his brother Frank were known to
enjoy their family ties and often visited both their close and
distant relatives when their travels took them to various
regions around the nation. Not only did these wanted outlaws often find a safe retreat with relatives, their national popularity made their visits an honor for such kin. On such
occasions it is reasonable to assume that such family members wanted photos made with their famous relatives. Usually
trusting their blood kin to keep their identity a secret and

copies of any such photos out of the hands of authorities, the James brothers apparently enjoyed such photo sessions with family members.

Although all of the known authentic photos that existed within the immediate James family have been found and preserved, it is reasonable to assume that others may still exist as unidentified family photos in attic trunks. In fact, the last two photos of Jesse James surfaced as late as 1992, and neither of these were within the family. In one Jesse and Frank James are standing in a group of employees at a Nashville, Tennessee, cedar bucket plant where they were employed for a brief period. The other was in the family of Kathryn Barnard in Oklahoma. Descended from Louis Washington Tapp, Kathryn heard stories within the family that the Tapps were neighbors and friends with the James family in Missouri. Including these last two photographs, sixteen images have been fully authenticated as being those of Jesse James by using George Warfel's image identification techniques.

George Warfel is a native of the Kansas City, Missouri, region and grew up hearing fascinating stories about Jesse James. He even had occasion in his youth to know and interview a gentleman who had actually known Jesse James as his neighbor Tom Howard in St. Joseph, Missouri. George's interest in the subject therefore began at an early age.

Because of his reputation as a well-known portrait artist and illustrator, Warfel was sought out by Milton F. Perry, the late James historian and Superintendent of Clay County, Missouri, Historic Sites, which included the James Farm Museum. Warfel was asked to assist in authenticating the dozens of family photographs the museum had received from the James family. His work with this endeavor began in 1981.

Although Warfel developed his own identification techniques, he later learned that his procedures were similar to those developed in the early 1900s by a Frenchman named Bertillon. Basically, the Warfel methods encompass four simple steps that are further aided by the fact that Warfel has spent more than fifty years as an artist and illustrator. This experience enables him to view the human anatomy with a more critical sense of proportion and detail than the average person possesses. Warfel realizes, however, that his procedures are subject to human error. But they have only failed once during the past twenty years of studying James family images.

First, upon receipt of a questionable photograph or special request for an opinion, enlargements of the subject's head are made measuring ten inches from the top of the head to the bottom of the chin. This enlargement is then mounted and covered with a sheet of velum tracing paper. A simple but accurate line tracing is then created. Horizontal lines are then carefully drawn across the facial, neck, and shoulder features. If the measurements between the lines then tally with the measurements made from one of the sixteen authenticated images, odds are in favor of the photo being a genuine one. These procedures work even better when both a frontal and profile photo made at the same level are available.

Further studies of ear cartilage, hairline, nose, nostrils, mouth, lips, neck, chin, and shoulder muscles using a special caliper instrument for measurements complete the process.

An alternative method to such procedures is to have positive transparencies made of the image being examined and placed over a transparency of an authenticated photo on a light table. Whether or not the feature points match determines the final assessment of authenticity.

Being a professional artist, Warfel is well aware of expressions most often determined by the mouth and eyes of the subject. Seldom do both eyes ever convey the same expression characteristics. It is also generally found that right and left profiles differ considerably. No two individuals in the history of mankind have ever been known to have exactly the same anatomy or expressions on both sides. Even identical twins may at first glance appear to be identical, but closer review will generally find major differences in certain anatomical, expression, and personality nuances that further affect appearance.

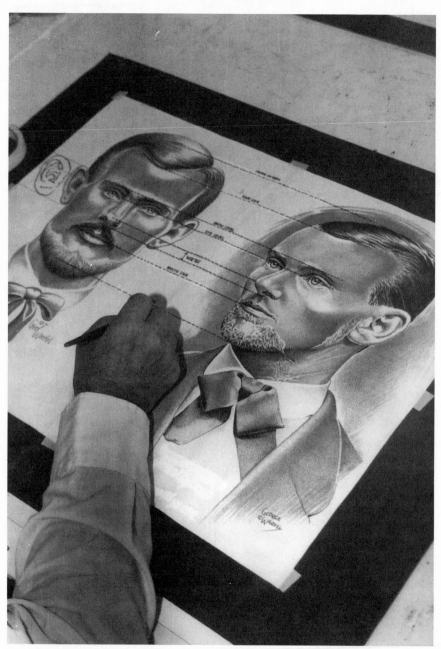

An example of the procedure George Warfel follows in determining the authenticity of a Jesse James photo or illustration.

NOTABLE PHYSICAL CHARACTERISTICS OF JESSE JAMES

A visual aid in determining authenticity of those photos claimed to be of Jesse James.

Other than the line drawing measurements, it is important to learn as much as possible about an individual's personality characteristics. Personality, or a person's inner being, definitely contributes to one's expressions and features. Recognizing how this affects persona, Warfel has studied numerous biographies of Jesse James, but even more importantly, he has learned about Jesse's personality through his close relationship to the James family over the years. James family descendants have all recognized the importance of preserving memories passed down in their family about their infamous ancestors. Such family records tell of Jesse James' strongest feature being his soul-piercing, crystal blue eyes. Sensitive to light, Jesse was known to blink often and experienced a granulated eyelid condition that occasionally caused swelling. Family memories further describe Jesse James as being a relatively small person at five feet, nine inches in height with small hands and feet (size 7½). The continual health problems caused by his right lung wounds during the Civil War are apparent in most of his authentic photographs. The condition of his health when a photo was made is easily recognizable since his weight fluctuated between 135 and 150 pounds.

The family further records Jesse James' personality as being most likeable; he was somewhat of a practical joker and extroverted; all of these characteristics made him a natural leader of men. He furthermore has been described as being a person whose pleasant attitude could turn instantly to deadly rage when provoked or faced with an injustice.

Jesse James' pride, which grew to be somewhat egotistical, is the trait most commonly recalled within the James family. He enjoyed dressing immaculately in the latest styles of the day and was constantly aware of his appearance both before the camera and in daily life. This concern for his appearance possibly provided Jesse James with an unplanned disguise because lawmen did not expect such a noted outlaw to have a manicured and businesslike appearance.

During his youth, Jesse James accidently shot off the tip of his middle left-hand finger in a gun accident. His self-consciousness over his mangled finger is clearly visible in all authentic photos of him. It is interesting to note that his left-hand fingers are carefully curled away from camera view by clutching his lapel or coat, if not hidden completely in a coat pocket.

Certain past James authors have indicated—in error—that Jesse James was left-handed. This may have come from the fact that often photo images were reversed in the development and duplication processes. Such reversals made it appear that the right hand was the left hand, hair was parted on the wrong side, and coat buttons were not placed properly.

The Warfel identification process, which has been perfected over the past twenty years, and his fifty years of studying human anatomy have resulted in his procedures being the most acceptable method of authenticating photo images of Jesse James. Regretfully, numerous highly respected books, magazines, and newspapers have published photos of Jesse James over the years that are not accurate. It is not the purpose of this text to discredit any of these publications, but rather to point out that those photo images used simply do not pass the Warfel identification procedures. It is furthermore hoped that future authors and publications will use more care in selecting photos for historical accuracy.

A few of the most commonly used images of Jesse James that have been proven to be inaccurate follow.

Commonly Used False Photos
of Jesse James

Although the man on the left in this photo closely resembles Jesse James at first glance, further review proves it is not Jesse. Jesse's nose is smaller, and this man's nose lacks the tilt evident in authenticated photos. This gentleman's eyes are too close together and do not have the correct slant. Jesse's chin is more prominent, and his feet are much smaller than this man's. The gentleman on the right is also not Jesse's brother Frank James for several reasons. (Author's collection)

This group photo from the Library of Congress has often been published as being Jesse and Frank James with a cousin Dingus James and Cole Younger. There is absolutely no resemblance whatsoever to authentic photos of the James or Younger brothers. It is believed to be a group of friends on a hunting trip who decided to jokingly portray the James-Younger brothers in a studio costume shop. (Author's collection)

Supposedly, this photo portrays Jesse James, left, and two of his gang members, neither of whom bears the slightest resemblance to his known associates. The Jesse James in this photo is far too tall, and his anatomical structure does not tally in any way with that of Jesse James in authentic photos. The boot size of this gentleman is much larger than the small 7½ size Jesse James wore. The man's forehead is too high, his ears are too long, and his eyes have a different slant. Further proving it could not be Jesse James, the two rifles the gentlemen to the right are holding were not manufactured until 1886—Jesse died in 1882. (Author's collection)

This photo was once being circulated in a "we-never-sleep" Pinkerton Detective Agency museum exhibit as being of Frank and Jesse James. It is small wonder that the Pinkerton Agency could never find the James brothers for there is no resemblance whatsoever of these men to the real Jesse and Frank James. Jesse James, supposedly the man standing, is at least 3½ inches taller than the real Jesse, and the anatomy of his hands and feet is not that of Jesse. Also, Jesse's 7½ boot size is much smaller than this man's. (Author's collection)

This is the most flagrantly false photo ever published as being Frank James, left, and Jesse James, right. Photo editors who used this picture, which originally came from Colorado, simply did not compare it to any of the James family authenticated photos. Comparison of this photo to any of the authenticated photos published here proves easily that it is not of the James brothers. (Author's collection)

This photo has on occasion been featured as Frank and Jesse James. The man purported to be Frank James on the left bears no resemblance at all to photos of the real Frank. Although the man on the right bears some resemblance to Jesse James, his forehead is too low, and his nose does not have the same tilt that Jesse's had. His chin is too short, and his jaws are too square for him to be Jesse James. This man somewhat resembles the J. Frank Dalton who claimed to be Jesse James still alive at age 101. (Author's collection)

CHAPTER 4

Jesse James Imposters

Jesse James had become a favorite personality of dime novel, police gazette, and newspaper readers long before that fateful morning of April 3, 1882. It was, therefore, a natural reaction for his admirers to disbelieve the newspaper headlines announcing the death of this notorious outlaw throughout the nation. The fact that their beloved Jesse James had survived the outlaw trail for some seventeen years through his extreme caution made the story of being shot from behind while unarmed simply unacceptable. Certainly this bold leader of the James-Younger gang would not have placed himself in such a position. Had Jesse been brought down in a hail of bullets from a lawman's posse or while escaping from a bank or train robbery, his admiring public would have found the story of his death more believable.

Furthermore, this was not the first time newspapers had reported that Jesse James was dead. George Shepard had left the James-Younger gang shortly after Jesse James shot and killed his nephew, Frank Shepard. George then married a Widow Maddox and attempted to live an honest life for some thirteen years, although he continued to be extremely bitter over the death of his nephew. Major Liggett, a Kansas City marshal, was aware of this bitterness and succeeded in convincing Shepard to become an informer.

Shepard regained Jesse's confidence and once again was accepted as a gang member in 1879. Jesse was making plans to rob the Stewart and MacArthur Bank in Short Creek, Missouri. Shepard had informed Marshal Liggett of the plan and, while riding into Short Creek on the day they planned the robbery, he carefully dropped back from the rest of the party in case Liggett's posse showed up. Noting an unusual number of soldiers around the community, Jesse cancelled the robbery plans and rode on through town.

As the party reached the outskirts of the city, Shepard's frustration exploded. Stopping his horse, he yelled out to Jesse, "You had no right to kill my nephew, Jesse James, and it's time his death was avenged!" Just as Jesse turned his horse, Shepard fired. Rolling off his horse, Jesse had escaped being hit, but Shepard didn't know that. Gang member Jim Cummins then ran down Shepard. Cummins received a bullet in the side, which fractured a rib, and Shepard caught a bullet in the right leg. Shepard's report to Marshal Liggett that he had killed Jesse James was a false one, but it did make newspaper headlines.

Because the Shepard story had been proven false and because the account of Jesse's death was in no way glamorous, rumors that it was another hoax began circulating shortly after his actual death. Because he was highly wanted with large rewards being offered for his capture, a clever hoax would have provided Jesse with a way to finally become a normal citizen and lead a peaceful life with his family. As reported in previous chapters, the evidence determined by the coroner's examination and coroner's jury proved beyond any doubt whatsoever that the bandit Jesse Woodson James was killed by a bullet from Bob Ford's gun as reported. Dozens of James family members and hundreds who had known Jesse or served with him during the Civil War had occasion to view his body both in St. Joseph, Missouri, and later at the Kearney House in Kearney before his burial. Not one single question was raised about the identity of the body.

The public, however, did not want to believe that Jesse James had truly left this world. An opportunity was therefore provided for several old men to later create stories of actually being the real and only Jesse James, who had skillfully survived the grave through a clever hoax.

The first such hoaxer seems to have been one John James. Little is known of this man's origins. He first became acquainted with the Reverend Robert E. Highley while, using the name Jesse James, he performed rope tricks on stage in small California towns. James apparently somehow convinced Highley that he truly was Jesse Woodson James.

John James later shows up operating as a horse trader in Illinois in 1926. He borrowed fifty cents from a twenty-two-year-old Charles Shelton. A few days later, Shelton asked for his money back and made public threats to the then seventy-nine-year-old gentleman. John James then shot

John James, who died in an Arkansas mental hospital in 1947, claimed to be Jesse James. He was promoted by the Reverend Robert E. Highley. (Author's collection)

and killed Shelton with a .38 caliber revolver. The murder charge against James was reduced to manslaughter. James pleaded guilty and received a one year-to-life sentence in the Menard, Illinois, prison. After serving one year, he was paroled to a Kentucky parole officer who later reported that James disappeared after having visited him as scheduled for eight times.

Apparently, John James read extensively about Jesse James during his year in prison, because soon after his parole, he once again assumed the name of Jesse James. He perhaps even began believing that he truly was Jesse and created a most intriguing story about how he had faked his death. It seems that a Missouri outlaw, Charles Bigelow, was close in size and appearance to Jesse James and had often robbed banks around the Midwest with the Thad gang. To avoid reprisal from the law, Bigelow would make sure everyone thought he was Jesse James before leaving the robbery site.

According to John James, Jesse schemed to escape into another life because he desired to leave his outlaw career and settle with his family on a Nebraska farm. Extremely bitter that Bigelow was furthering his outlaw reputation and causing the rewards for his capture to increase, Jesse planned to capture and kill Bigelow. Supposedly, Jesse and his friends then found and killed Bigelow early on the morning of April 3, 1882. His body was then brought into Jesse's St. Joseph home and laid out on the parlor floor. Jesse's wife Zee covered her dress with chicken blood and held the dead Bigelow in her arms until authorities arrived. Desiring for his Ford brother friends to get the reward being offered, Jesse arranged for Bob Ford to shoot a hole in the wall and with his brother Charley Ford run to tell the world they had killed Jesse James. Jesse's wife, mother, relatives, and associates were all in on the plot and identified the body of Bigelow as being poor Jesse. According to John James, the real Jesse James then left for Argentina where he would spend several years as a free man before returning to America.

Although the man's story was quite preposterous, there were those who wanted to believe him. John James seemed to be quite knowledgeable of James history and apparently was quite convincing when questioned by reporters. Learning of the old man's story, promoters began arranging lecture tours for him. One such lecture in Excelsior Springs, Missouri, was advertised to be by Jesse James—who had survived the grave. The auditorium was filled to capacity. After "James" had completed his lecture, a lady in the audience stood up and exclaimed loudly, "If you truly are Jesse James, I have a pair of Jesse's boots here for you to try on." The boots were size 7½, and John James' large feet would not fit into them. The lady was none other than Annie James, Frank James' wife. John James was laughed off the stage and run out of town.

The Reverend Robert E. Highley, known as "The Flying Preacher" had remembered James from California and, upon James' release from prison, returned to Missouri to re-establish his relationship with him. Apparently feeling that "Jesse James Alive" could help draw crowds to his "fire and brimstone" revivals around the Midwest, Highley employed John James for a period.

Again in Excelsior Springs, Missouri, John James asked to spend the night in jail there in 1933. Frank James' son Robert heard that the old man had almost convinced the sheriff there that he was truly Jesse James. Robert then visited the jail and easily proved him to be a fake with a number of questions he could not answer. One was about Jesse's young half-brother Archie Peyton Samuel. James did not know the boy's middle name.

Highley took John James the next day to visit Jesse James' only daughter, Mary Susan, who had married Henry Lafayette Barr and lived in Kearney, Missouri. Mary refused to meet the man and hid herself in a bedroom during his visit. Highley later reported in a book he had published in 1981 that Mr. Barr asked James several questions only Jesse could have answered. The fact that he answered them correctly, according to Highley, convinced Henry Barr of the man's authenticity. John James died in the Arkansas State Mental Hospital on December 24, 1947. Had he truly been the real Jesse James, he would have been age 100 at his death.

Certainly by now the years alone would have prevented any other such hoaxer to claim to be Jesse James still alive. As might be expected, however, Orvus Lee Howk saw a way to further stretch Jesse's life for four more years. In 1948, Howk, claiming to be the grandson of Jesse James—and that his own name was really Jesse Lee James III—brought forth Jesse James at age 101 in Lawton, Oklahoma. Newspaper headlines flashed the phenomenal story around the world.

Howk, who was apparently aware of the story his predecessor John James had told, had discovered J. Frank Dalton and trained him thoroughly with the story John James had previously used.

Noted Old West historian and rare book dealer Ed Bartholomew of Fort Davis, Texas, reported that he first met J. Frank Dalton during an old-timers' convention at the White Plaza Hotel in Corpus Christi, Texas, in 1933. Dressed in a white suit with white shoes, the man

Orvus Lee Howk (Jesse Lee James III) claimed to be the grandson of J. Frank Dalton, whom he promoted as being Jesse Woodson James, still alive in 1948. (Photo by author)

was calling himself at that time "The Kid." Bartholomew further recalled that the *Caller-Times* newspaper featured a story at the time about Dalton's possibly being "Billy the Kid." Bartholomew later knew Dalton as a regular around the cafes, taverns, and oil boomtowns Kilgore, Gladewater, Henderson, and others in East Texas during the 1930s. During this period, Dalton often wrote articles about various Old West subjects for newspapers of the region while he worked at odd jobs in the oil fields. Dalton also was often seen working as a carnival roustabout with traveling carnivals around East Texas. Bartholomew further recalls first meeting Orvus Howk with Dalton in an East Texas cafe in 1939.

No doubt feeling that J. Frank Dalton fit the right age and appearance, Howk chose him to be Jesse James still alive and to somehow capitalize on the hoax. Bartholomew recalls that Howk was one of his best book customers and bought every book he could find about Jesse James.

Although there are many theories as to the true identity of J. Frank Dalton, he still remains a mystery. In 1938, while attempting to file an application for a Confederate pension, Dalton claimed that he was born on March 8, 1848, in Galiad, Texas. He further claimed that his father had been a colonel in the U.S. Army and served in the Mexican War. Because neither Texas state records nor federal records, however, confirmed this, his pension was declined, and he was ready to accept being promoted as Jesse James to earn a livelihood.

Howk first took the old man to Lawton, Oklahoma, where, in 1948, he convinced newspaper man Robert C. Ruark that this was Jesse James, still alive at age 101. Newspaper headlines featured the story throughout the nation.

Noted James author Homer Croy went to Lawton, where he met Dalton in the Highway Hotel. Despite Croy's proof that Dalton was not Jesse James when he failed miserably to answer Croy's questions, Howk continued his promotion of Dalton as Jesse. CBS asked Ruark and Croy to come to New York where their debate regarding whether or not J. Frank

J. Frank Dalton, right, with Al Jennings, claimed to be Jesse James still alive in 1948. (Author's collection)

Dalton was Jesse James was broadcast nationally. Hearing about the man's story, Rudy Turilli of Stanton, Missouri, created a major promotion plan for Meramec Caverns, which was a major tourist attraction near Stanton, Missouri.

Learning of the story Howk and Dalton were telling, Turilli created a tremendous amount of publicity for their cavern attraction by arranging to bring Dalton, as Jesse James, to Stanton for Jesse James' 103rd birthday party on September 5, 1950. Featuring Jesse James' return to his old hideout for his birthday created national media exposure for the caverns. Not only did Turilli bring Jesse James, but he also found Cole Younger (alias James R. Davis), still alive at age 106, in Nashville, Tennessee, and arranged for him to come to the caverns for the celebration. Davis, like Dalton,

J. Frank Dalton claimed to be Jesse James at age 102 in 1950. (Author's collection)

also told a preposterous tale of how he had traded places and paid another man to be Cole Younger and serve his sentence in the Minnesota State Prison. John Trammell, who claimed to have known Jesse James and Cole Younger when he cooked for the gang, was found alive at age 110 in Oklahoma and was also brought to Stanton where he positively identified the two old outlaws as being who they claimed to be. Al Jennings, the Oklahoma bank robber of the 1930s, also was brought for the party but never identified Dalton as Jesse James.

Although somewhat knowledgeable, which several skeptics found to be impressive, Howk pointed out that Dalton's index finger on his left hand was mutilated. He apparently slipped here because it was the middle finger on Jesse's left hand that had been damaged in a gun accident and not the index finger. Explaining why there were no chest wound scars on Dalton's body, Howk said they were repaired by skin grafting.

No doubt achieving a great deal of national publicity from his Jesse-James-alive-at-Meramec-Caverns stunt, Rudy Turilli later told the story of Dalton being Jesse James in his book *The Truth about Jesse James* in 1966. In the book, Turilli offered a $10,000 reward to anyone who could prove that J. Frank Dalton was not the one and only Jesse Woodson James, outlaw. Stella James, wife of Jesse James' only son, Jesse Edwards

James, and Ethel Rose Owens and Estelle Baumel, grandchildren of Jesse James, challenged Turilli in court. The case was tried in the Franklin County, Missouri, Circuit Court in May of 1970. Turilli lost the case and was ordered by the judge to pay the relatives of Jesse James $10,000. Turilli then sought to appeal the case in the St. Louis Court of Appeals, but again lost. Turilli died in 1972 without ever paying the judgment.

Meanwhile, J. Frank Dalton had died in Granbury, Texas, on August 15, 1951. Howk along with Ola M. Everhard, who had been Dalton's nurse and claimed to be his cousin, further perpetuated the hoax by erecting a monument on Dalton's grave that reads, "Jesse Woodson James, Sept. 5, 1847–Aug. 15, 1951, supposedly killed in 1882."

Just who this J. Frank Dalton really was remains somewhat of a mystery. The fact that he definitely was not Jesse James was firmly established in 1986 when documented handwriting of Jesse James was compared with known writing of J. Frank Dalton. Howard Chandler of Questioned Documents Examiner Associates in Little Rock, Arkansas, stated after an in-depth analysis, "We are unable to identify the known handwriting of Jesse James in the letter of April 16, 1880, with the handwriting of J. Frank Dalton."

Dalton certainly was most knowledgeable on James, Younger, and Quantrill guerilla forces history. Most researchers feel the man may have actually served with guerilla forces during the Civil War and knew the James story well but was definitely not the Jesse Woodson James we know from Old West history. One clue to his possible identity came from Myrtle Abendroth of Kansas, who claimed to have known Jerrimiah Franklin Dalton of Lansing, Kansas, in his youth. She also recalled that this J. Frank Dalton often used the alias of Dolby or Darby. Ed Bartholomew confirmed that when he first knew J. Frank Dalton, he used the Dolby alias. If J. Frank Dalton was this Jerrimiah, census records reflect that Dalton would have been age 87 upon his death and not 104. Jerremiah Franklin Dalton was the son of William Clark Meredith Dalton and

Believed to be J. Frank Dalton at an early age. Often using the aliases of Dolby and Darby, he did not claim to be Jesse James until 1948. (Courtesy of Myrtle Abendroth)

Josephine Morris. Records indicate he was born in Lansing, Kansas, in 1864, and married Andrea Anderson. However, because death records indicate that the man known as Darby died in Belleville, Kansas, August 3, 1947, it is doubtful Jerrimiah was J. Frank Dalton.

As for Orvus Lee Howk, alias Jesse Lee James III, he once reported to this author that there were two sets of James brothers who were cousins. He stated that George James, a brother to the Reverend Robert James, father of Jesse, Frank, and Susan James of Missouri, had children Sylvester Franklin and Jesse Woodson in Scott County, Kentucky. This Kentucky Jesse had a son Jesse Barnhill James, who was the father of Jesse Lee James III. Howk further explained that George James, brother of Robert James, did not appear on U.S. census records because he was the oldest child and away from home when the census was taken. Howk's crude attempt to prove his story of being the grandson of Jesse James failed dismally because no record anywhere in Kentucky reveals any such George James family.

When Stella James, wife of Jesse James' only son was once asked about Jesse Lee James III, she commented, "There was no Jesse James III. If there had been, he would have been my child, and I had no son."

Howk's wild tales further attempted to explain why he used the name Orvus Lee Howk if his real name was Jesse Lee

James III. He explained that after his grandfather, Jesse James, returned to America from South America, he became extremely wealthy from his investments in coal mining, oil, railroads, and the movie industry. According to Howk, old Jesse was even once a partner with Howard Hughes in Hughes Tool Company and RKO Studios. As a result of this wealth, young Jesse III was kidnapped at age 4 and held for a large ransom that his grandfather paid. Thereafter, to prevent future kidnapping attempts, young Jesse III was sent to live with relatives, Mr. and Mrs. Obediah Howk of St. Louis, and he took the name of Orvus Howk.

Howk further promoted the hoax long after J. Frank Dalton died by telling of the many treasures his grandfather had been aware of; they were hidden throughout the Southwest by the Knights of the Golden Circle organization his grandfather Jesse James had belonged to. This secret society supposedly had accumulated huge amounts of gold and buried the gold in secret places to later be recovered to re-arm the South to start the Civil War over again. Howk claimed to have old secret maps to these treasure locations, so his stories continued to excite imaginations and no doubt sent many treasure hunters off on unprofitable adventures. The last such treasure hunt using Howk's old maps was directed by Howk's two sons in Waco, Texas, in 1992. Although many months and dollars were spent on the Waco project, no treasure was ever found.

Orvus Lee Howk died in the mid-1980s while visiting a friend and believer of his stories in Scottsdale, Arizona. Although author Phillip Steele interviewed Orvus Howk on several occasions when he was living in Rogers, Arkansas, in 1983, with his sons Jesse Lee James IV and Woodson James, Howk's true identity still remains a mystery. One theory suggests that perhaps J. Frank Dalton was really Obediah Howk from St. Louis and truly was the grandfather of Orvus Howk. It was simply more fun to be the grandson of Jesse James, so the hoax was created.

Although the stories told by John James, J. Franklin Dalton, and Orvus Howk were the ones that created the most books and newsprint, they were not the only two who claimed to be Jesse James long after Jesse's death in 1882. The family of William H. Parmley of Locust Grove, Oklahoma, firmly believe that Parmley was Jesse James. Their story tells that Parmley served during the Civil War from November 1863 to July of 1865. He died August 27, 1906, in Newton County, Missouri, from wounds received during the war. An old family Bible led the family to believe that the man was actually Jesse James, who had traded names with William Parmley in a tangled and incomprehensible story.

Vincel Simmons of Missouri first questioned the fact that Jesse James was truly killed in 1882 when a relative, Elizabeth James, approached him in 1976. This mysterious Elizabeth James left a box of old photos, gold coins, and other items with Simmons that led him to believe that his grandparents, Jacob and Miriam Gerlt, may have actually been Jesse and Zee James. Apparently feeling that people in many of the old photographs resembled Jesse James, Zee James, or possibly J. Frank Dalton, he began further researching the James story. Jacob Gerlt died in 1950. If he could have been Jesse James, Gerlt would have been age 103 at his death. Since J. Frank Dalton died in 1951, Gerlt could not have been Dalton. Because he claimed to be the grandson of Jesse James, Simmons' story was published by *Ozark Life,* Mountain Home, Arkansas, in a book entitled *Jesse James: The Real Story* in 1994. None of the photos found in Simmons' collection resemble documented photos of the James family in any way. The Vincel Simmons story therefore must be considered only as folklore, along with all the other such hoaxes that have surfaced since Jesse James' death in 1882.

The fact so many elderly gentlemen sought notoriety by creating such claims of being Jesse James might be explained in a statement made by Dr. David Williams, a psychiatrist with the Ozark Guidance Center in Washington County, Arkansas. He stated that age often alters reality. Older men sometimes will compensate for dull lives, fulfill their need for attention, or simply enjoy becoming someone else by telling these larger-than-life stories about themselves. Such men often may actually become who they imagine and truly believe the stories they tell.

Jesse's brother Frank James died of natural causes on the James farm in Kearney, Missouri, on February 15, 1915. Three men—one in Moccasin Bend, Tennessee; one in Tacoma, Washington; and one in Wayton, Arkansas—claimed to be the one and only Frank James even before Frank's wife Annie died on July 6, 1944.

The stories told by the hoaxers covered in this chapter should by no means ever be confused with documented history. They are reported here only as examples of the volumes of folklore created by the James story. The authors here firmly believe, as will any dedicated researcher, that Jesse Woodson James died at age 34 from a bullet to the back of the head on April 3, 1882, and that his remains are interred in the Mt. Olivet Cemetery in Kearney, Missouri.

CHAPTER 5

Portraits of Jesse

While a student at the Kansas City Art Institute, George Warfel was greatly influenced by one of his instructors, Thomas Hart Benton, who not only shared his techniques of portrait art with his students but also encouraged George to continue his interest in Missouri history and the period dealing with the James story. One of Benton's most famous murals in the Missouri State Capitol in Jefferson City features Jesse James in the act of robbing a train. It occurred to Warfel that if his noted mentor took satisfaction in rendering illustrations of Jesse James and other outlaws, perhaps he could also. Warfel therefore continued where Benton left off.

From this training at the Kansas City Art Institute and the Corcoran School of Art in Washington, D.C., Warfel's career in the graphics art field progressed. Before his retirement, he held numerous positions as the art director for several government agencies and he was also the staff director for art instructors at Columbia Technical Institute, a Washington, D.C., trade school.

Warfel has rendered portraits of numerous well-known personalities of the Old West. One exhibit—the largest one of its kind in existence—which contains 42 life-sized portraits, has been on display since 1983 in the Patee House Museum in St. Joseph, Missouri. His main concentration in this subject matter, however, is on Jesse and Frank James. He has spent nearly sixty years of association with members of the James family—beginning in 1937 with Jo Frances James, a granddaughter of Jesse James, and continuing to the present with Mrs. Lawrence Barr (Thelma) and her daughter, Betty Barr, great-granddaughter of Jesse; and Superior Court Judge James R. Ross, of Orange County, California, the great-grandson of Jesse James. Warfel has often stated that without their inspiration and help he could never have rendered portraits of the James brothers so convincingly. Their disclosures of the brothers' activities and personalities and access to their family albums helped him immeasurably in rendering his images accurately. Added to this were the descriptions obtained from two residents of St. Joseph in the early 1930s by a much younger George Warfel. An elderly man and woman who knew Jesse as "Mr. Howard" gave detailed reports of his physical appearance and mannerisms.

No other artist, living or dead, has rendered the number of portraits of Frank and Jesse James that George Warfel has. The curators of the museums at Kearney, Liberty, and St. Joseph, Missouri, where his works are displayed, believe the Warfel portraits to be the the most accurately rendered portraits of the two brothers in existence. Examples of the Warfel portraits of Jesse James that best portray his true appearance and personality follow.

Jesse James, The Boy, 1862. *Rendered from the earliest known photograph of Jesse taken in a Kansas City studio, this image of Jesse James clearly indicates his youthful innocence before the tides of the Civil War swept over his family. He had not yet experienced the severe beating in the field or the hanging of his stepfather by Union authorities. These mistakes eventually would cost the state of Missouri many lives and dollars as this wayward lad's life turned into one of vengeance.*

Jesse James, The Rebel, 1864. *This portrait of Jesse James was rendered from an original ambrotype photograph taken in Platte City, Missouri, on July 10, 1864, when Quantrill's forces attacked the town. He had joined Quantrill's forces in the spring of 1864 and this image expresses the smoldering temperment within him that developed as a result of the many injustices suffered by his family.*

Jesse James, The Wounded Soldier, 1865. *Seeking treatment from a lung wound he had received while attempting to surrender under a white flag in Missouri, Jesse James returned to Nashville, Tennessee. This portrait, rendered from the original photograph taken in Nashville, Tennessee, in 1866, when Jesse was 18 years old, clearly reveals his weight loss and his attitude as a result of the war.* (Original photo from the Mamie Pence collection)

Jesse James, The Bandit. *His photograph in Greenville, Illinois, from which this portrait was created, indicates that Jesse had fully recovered from his war wounds and by now had become the gentleman bank robber who had never fully accepted the defeat of the Confederate cause.*

Jesse James, The Gentleman Outlaw. *Rendered from the photograph
taken in Long Branch, New Jersey, in 1871, when Jesse was 23 years old.
Jesse enjoyed the good life there in Long Branch and at Saratoga Springs,
New York, while lawmen searched for the outlaws in Mid-America.*

Jesse James, Train Robber, 1873. *By now this veteran bank and stagecoach robber, Jesse James, found peace around racetracks in Clarinda, Iowa, where the photograph from which this portrait was made was taken. Soon afterward, he would be credited for inventing train robbery.* (Photograph for this portrait courtesy of Erich Bauman)

Gentleman from Missouri, 1873. *This illustration was rendered from studies of several photographs taken in the early 1870s.*

Jesse James, The Peak of His Career. *Rendered from the photograph taken in Nebraska City, Nebraska, in 1875, when Jesse was 28 years old (the most widely circulated photo of Jesse through the years). This was the same year in which the Pinkerton Detective Agency bombed his farm home—an incident that killed his half-brother Archie Samuel, maimed his mother, and caused Jesse James' bitterness to grow.*

Dingus at Northfield. *As Jesse appeared in September 1876 while at the fiasco in Northfield, Minnesota. This is an exact likeness, however it is an illustration rendered from studies of several photographs taken in the 1870s, near the time of the incident. The dress is appropriate according to Northfield residents' descriptions given at that time.*

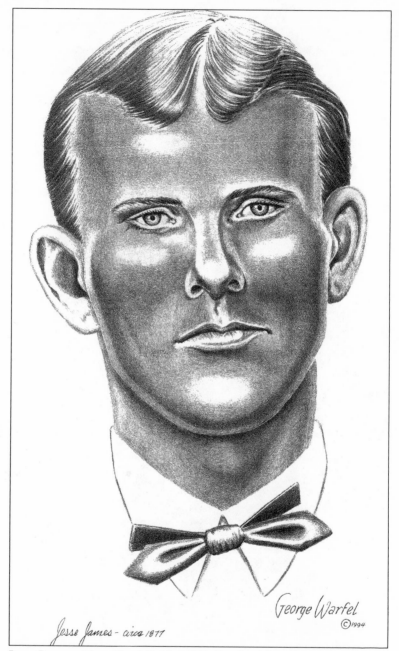

Jesse James - circa 1877

George Warfel
©1994

Jesse James, After Northfield, 1877. *Rendered from a combination of photo images of Jesse James between the period of 1876 to 1878, this is how the stylish survivor of the unfortunate Northfield raid would have appeared. Jesse's age here is about 30 years old.*

Jesse James, Nashville Businessman, 1880. *Settling with their families in Nashville, Tennessee, after the ill-fated Northfield raid, the James brothers attempted to blend into Nashville society as businessmen. This illustration is rendered from the photograph taken in Nashville, Tennessee, in 1880, when Jesse was approximately 32 years old.*

Jesse James, Return to Missouri, 1881. *Fearing detection when one of the gang members was captured near Nashville, Jesse James returned with his family to Kansas City while his brother Frank drifted into Alabama and later Virginia. This portrait, based on descriptions at the time, reveals how Jesse James, as Tom Howard, businessman, appeared at the time. It is rendered from the study of several group photographs and singling out Jesse from the others; the photos were taken between 1875 and 1882. This is circa 1880, when he was about 33 years old.*

This image is rendered from the study of death photographs taken at Sidenfaden's Funeral Parlor, St. Joseph, Missouri, in 1882 and from photos taken in 1873 and 1875. Here, Jesse is approximately 34 years old.

Jesse James, [alias] Thomas Howard of St. Joseph, 1882. *This rendering taken from photographs made of his corpse in St. Joseph, Missouri, on April 3, 1882, portrays the image of Jesse James as Thomas Howard, businessman, shortly before two gang members seeking the reward for Jesse's capture murdered him.* (Use of portrait courtesy of Gary Chilcote, Patee House Museum, St. Joseph, Missouri.)

Bibliography

BOOKS

Black, Hugh. *History of John and Susanna Cole of Culpepper County, Virginia.* N.p., n.d.

Brant, Marley. *The Outlaw Youngers: A Confederate Brotherhood: A Biography.* Lanham, MD: Madison Books, 1992.

James, James Edwards. *Jesse James, My Father.* Cleveland, OH: The Arthur Westbrook Company, 1906.
Written by the only son of Jesse James.

James, Stella Francis. *In the Shadow of Jesse James.* N. p.: The Revolver Press, a division of Dragon Books, 1990.

Love, Robertus. *The Rise and Fall of Jesse James.* New York: G. P. Putnam and Sons, 1926.

Ross, James R. *I, Jesse James.* N.p.: Dragon Publishing Corporation, 1989.
Written by the great-grandson of Jesse James.

Settle, William A., Jr. *Jesse James Was His Name; or, Fact and Fiction Concerning the Careers of the Notorious James Brothers of Missouri.* Lincoln, NE: University of Nebraska Press, 1977.

Steele, Phillip W. *Jesse and Frank James: The Family History.* Gretna, LA: Pelican, 1987.

Wymore, Jack. *Goodbye Jesse James*. Liberty, Missouri: Jesse James Bank Museum, 1967.

Six major newspaper articles from 1882.

Yeatman, Ted, and Steve Eng. *Jesse James and Bill Ryan at Nashville.* Nashville: Nashville House, 1982.

MAGAZINES

Hoctor, Emmett. *NOLA Quarterly*. April-June 1992, October-December 1991.

Hundreds of newspapers and other records involved in this collection of information about Jesse and Frank James visits in Nebraska.

Owens, Amy. "Desperados and Aficionados." *The Blood-Horse* (January 1988).

Yeatman, Ted. "Jesse James in Tennessee." *NOLA Quarterly*.

NEWSPAPERS

Bates Co. News-Headliner. March 25, 1982; article by James Barnhart.

Hoctor, Emmett; collections of newspaper articles relating to Jesse and Frank James' visits in Nebraska.

Kansas City Star. Dec. 13, 1931; articles by A. B. Macdonald relating to Jesse James' death.

Nebraska State Journal, April 7, 1882.

St. Joseph Herald. April 6, 1882; April 7, 1882; April 9, 1882.

Weaver, Barry Roland. "Jesse James in Arkansas." *Arkansas Historical Society.* 23 (no. 4) (Winter 1964).

INTERVIEWS

Lawrence Barr (grandson of Jesse James), James Farm, Kearney, Mo., 1981.

Thelma Barr (wife of Lawrence Barr) Overland Park, Kan., 1981-1991.

Orvus Lee Howk (grandson of J. Frank Dalton), Rogers, Ark., 1979-80.

Ethel Rose Owens (granddaughter of Jesse James), James Farm, Kearney, Mo., and Kansas City, Mo., 1982.

Milton F. Perry (Superintendent, Clay County Historic Sites), Kansas City, Kearney, and Liberty, Mo., 1983-1991.

James R. Ross (great-grandson of Jesse James), Kansas City and Kearney, Mo., 1983-1991.

Dr. William A. Settle (author of *Jesse James Was His Name; or, Fact and Fiction Concerning the Careers of the Notorious James Brothers of Missouri*), Tulsa, Okla., and Kearney, Mo., 1983-88.

Vincel Simmons (grandson of Jacob Gerlt), Springdale, Ark., 1976, and St. Joseph, Mo., 1994.

RESEARCH ASSISTANCE

Lyle Reedstrom, Cedar Lake, Indiana

Lynda Snyder, Yorba Linda, California

SPECIAL ASSISTANCE

Jan Cooper, Fayetteville, Arkansas

Index

Index of Photos and Illustrations

Authors Phillip W. Steele, left, and George Warfel at the James farm home, 1994.

About the Authors

Phillip W. Steele of Springdale, Arkansas, and George Warfel first met at a James-Younger family reunion held in 1981 at the James farm, birthplace of Jesse James. Out of their many shared common interests, including separating the facts from the volumes of fiction written about Jesse James and his associates, their close relationship has grown.

Born in the "Hell-on-the-Border" city of Fort Smith, Arkansas, Steele grew up in the highlands of the northwest Arkansas Ozarks hearing his grandparents tell many stories of the region. Not only did they tell and retell the legends of the Ozarks, his grandfather loved to relate stories from his years spent as a cowboy in western Colorado. Steele, therefore, developed an interest in Ozark folklore and the Old West at an early age. Realizing he was only the third generation from the actual beginnings of such stories, as well as the fact that few of these legends and tales had ever been written down, he began writing of his heritage some thirty years ago.

Steele attended Kemper Military Academy, UCLA, and the University of Arkansas, from which he holds a B.S. degree. He joined his family's food processing business after college, where he continues to serve as President of Good Old Days Foods, Inc., of Springdale.

Steele's column, "Hearth Tales," appeared in the *Ozarks Mountaineer* magazine for some twelve years, thereby assuring preservation of many folktales of the region. He has had more than one hundred articles published on the Old West, Ozark folklore, and history published in magazines and newspapers. His published works by Pelican Publishing Company include *The Last Cherokee Warriors, Ozark Tales and Superstitions, Jesse and Frank James: The Family History, Starr Tracks: Belle and Pearl Starr, Outlaws and Gunfighters of the Old West,* and *Civil War in the Ozarks.* Other works by Heritage Publishing are *Butterfield Run* and *Lost Treasures of the Ozarks.*

In 1989, Steele formed Heritage Productions, which produces documentary films on Old West and Ozark folklore subjects for video release. He has hosted and narrated two such productions and is currently producing *The Haunted Hills* and *Belle Starr.*

Hearing many Ozark stories about Jesse James while growing up, Steele developed his fascination with the James history at an early age. He credits mentors Milton Perry and Dr. William Settle with inspiring his continual research and interest in Jesse James, the James-Younger gang, and the era represented by them in American history. Milton Perry served as the superintendent of Clay County, Missouri, Historic Sites for many years before his retirement and death in 1992. Dr. Settle of Tulsa, Oklahoma, spent many years researching the James-Younger story, which resulted in his highly respected book, *Jesse James Was His Name; or, Fact and Fiction Concerning the Careers of the Notorious James Brothers of Missouri.* Both Perry and Settle greatly influenced and assisted Steele in his early research of the James story.

Serving as president of Friends of the James Farm for two terms and currently serving as president of the James-Younger Gang, Steele developed a close relationship with many of the James-Younger family descendants. Such family friendships and advice have contributed greatly to this publication. Steele also is a member of Western Writers of America and serves on the board of directors of the National Outlaw and Lawman History Association. He also serves on the Arkansas History Commission board and the Arkansas Film Commission. Recognized as a leading authority on the James story, he consulted with the writers and producers on a recent film, *Frank and Jesse,* produced in Arkansas.

George Warfel was born in Kansas City, Missouri, and spent his early years in Sabetha, Kansas. Upon graduation from Paseo High School, he attended the Kansas City Art Institute, where he was privileged to know and receive instruction from the internationally renowned artist, Thomas Hart Benton. His art education continued at Corcoran

School of Art and the American University in Washington, D.C.

After serving from 1941 to 1945 with the Army Air Corps during World War II, he pursued his career with four government agencies, two commercial art firms, and as an instructor and director of Columbia Technical Institute, an art trade school in the Washington, D.C., area. Since his retirement in 1973, Warfel has concentrated on his western art. Portraits of more than forty-two personalities we know from the annals of Old West history make up his famous exhibit, which has been on display at the Patee House Museum in St. Joseph, Missouri, since 1983. This is the nation's largest such western portrait exhibit. His portraits are also on display at the James Farm Museum in Kearney, Missouri; the Liberty Bank Museum in Liberty, Missouri; and in other historic sites around the nation.

While he was staying with relatives in Shawnee Mission, Kansas, Warfel's interest in Jesse James, Quantrill's guerilla forces, and Old West history in general first began when he met William Elsey Connely, the famous Kansas historian. Listening to the wonderful tales Connely told, Warfel was fascinated. His lifelong interest in Jesse James and the era in American history he represents first began when he was ten years old. His first portrait of Jesse James was rendered in 1930 for a schoolteacher who shared his interest in the James story. The teacher's lavish praise of his work inspired him to continue what has become a lifetime of portrait art with a concentration on the James family and their true history.

George Warfel also cherishes experiences he had in 1934 at age sixteen with two old-timers who had actually known Jesse James and experienced Quantrill's bloody raid on Lawrence, Kansas. One had been a neighbor to Jesse and his family in St. Joseph, Missouri. Not realizing that Mr. Howard was in reality Jesse James, this neighbor and Jesse became good friends and often played cards together. The other old-timer was a Lawrence schoolteacher when Quantrill raided the city on August 21, 1863. Warfel carefully recorded the details shared in these interviews.

In 1937, George Warfel first met Jo Francis Ross, granddaughter of Jesse James, when she was writing the book on Jesse's life from which 20th Century Fox was planning their Jesse James film. George was asked to render several pieces of art for the book and was featured with Jo Francis in *Time-Life* magazine two years later. Starring Tyrone Power, Henry Fonda, Nancy Kelley, Randolph Scott, John Carradine, and others who were later to become major stars, the movie was filmed in Pineville, Missouri, in 1938. Warfel went to Pineville during the filming where he drew portraits of many of the stars. These portraits were subsequently used by Fox to promote the film. Later, they were rented to various theaters before the exhibit was destroyed in a theater fire in 1939. Warfel, therefore, credits Jesse James for his first income in the art field.

After his retirement in 1973, Warfel became close friends with Lawrence Barr, a grandson of Jesse James, and other family members, who shared their family photographs and history with him. He has since rendered numerous paintings of Jesse James and other family members based on such photographs, anatomy studies, personality traits, and guidance from descendants of Jesse James.

Over his some fifty years of researching and painting James portraits, George Warfel has developed his nearly flawless techniques of identifying James family photographs. He has since become the nation's best authority on James photographs and continues to serve the James Farm Museum and others as a consultant on questionable James family photographs as they are discovered.

George Warfel has served with Phillip Steele on the Friends of the James Farm board of directors for many years and they both currently serve on the James-Younger Gang board. Now residing in Venice, Florida, Warfel continues to enjoy his art and to provide his photo identification skills to museums and others seeking such documentation.